Find It
Buy It
Fix It

The Insider's Guide to Fixer-Uppers

Robert Irwin

**Real Estate
Education Company**
a division of Dearborn Financial Publishing, Inc.

Acquisitions Editor: Christine E. Litavsky
Managing Editor: Jack Kiburz
Interior Design: Lucy Jenkins
Cover Design: S. Laird Jenkins Corporation

Library of Congress Cataloging-in-Publication Data

Irwin, Robert, 1941–
    Find it, buy it, fix it : the insider's guide to fixer-uppers \ Robert Irwin.
        p. cu.
    Includes index.
    ISBN 0-7931-1630-9 (pbk.)
        1. House buying. 2. Dwellings—Remodeling. 3. Real estate investment. I. Title.
HD1379.I643   1996   95-42406
643'.12—dc20   CIP

Contents

CHAPTER 1

Do You Want a Fixer-Upper?

Most buyers really don't want fixer-uppers, also known as fixers or handyman's specials.

They may say they do, but as real estate agents and savvy sellers know, most buyers love to walk into a property and see that it has clean carpeting and repainted walls, and that everything looks good and is in working order. It's a truism in real estate that the house that looks good sells faster and for more money.

Yet, most buyers will still specifically ask about fixers. The reason? In a word, profit.

People believe (and it's true) that fixers cost much less than properties that are in ready-to-go shape. Consequently, when many buyers say they want a fixer, what they simply want is a reduced price (not the work that a fixer requires), so they can resell for much more. Unfortunately, these people rarely buy true fixers, because the moment they see the bad condition such places are in, they opt for something already fixed up.

You, however, are different. Chances are you already know that there's good money to be made in fixers, and you're not going to be scared away by the work to be done. (Either you'll do it yourself, or you'll hire it out.) What you really want to know is (1) how to find fixers, (2) how to buy them cheaply and (3) how to fix them up so they'll have sales appeal. It is no accident that this book is divided into three parts under just such headings.

In this book, we'll examine fixer-uppers from all angles. But first, let's consider some of the true benefits that fixers offer, benefits that sometimes aren't clearly seen. First, of course, there's making money.

Do You Want a Moneymaker?

Fixers or handyman's specials are to real estate what cars with scratched paint and dented fenders are to auto resales. They are a challenge and, very often, an opportunity.

Although a fixed-up house will bring top dollar and a quick sale, a run-down house will bring a lower price and take longer to sell. So, why not buy the run-down house, spend a few bucks to fix it up and then quickly resell for a profit? Why not indeed? The opportunity to make quick money is the most common reason given for looking at fixers.

Are You Looking for a Profit Center?

You have to live somewhere, so why not spend the next year or two living in a fixer, all the while improving it? For the industrious and handy, a live-in fixer can be a thriving, almost full-time business. It can be the chance to turn a residence into a profit center.

This is how it's often done: One spouse continues with a regular job, while the other is fixing up the house. By carefully budgeting time and money, the couple does many of the repairs, buys needed materials and handles other costs through mortgage borrowing, which is paid off on sale.

If done right, the buyers live virtually rent-free in the property. Plus, they've made a handsome profit.

Do You Want To Get into a Neighborhood You Couldn't Otherwise Afford?

The expression "champagne taste with a beer budget" applies to almost everyone who wants to buy real estate. It's simply because real estate (the land) is so expensive, particularly in the most desirable areas. We know *where* we want to live, but very often we simply can't afford to move into that neighborhood, at least not at market prices.

But, what if you could buy into that dream neighborhood for below market? Far below? You usually can, if you're willing to accept a handyman's special. At market price, you'll find a well-landscaped, pedicured home. But, in virtually every neighborhood there are those properties that, for whatever reason, owners have allowed to run down. They're the messes and the uglies. But because of that very fact, they're much less expensive.

You get in cheaper, often much cheaper. And, if you supply the labor, you may be able to fix up a handyman's special for only a fraction of your original purchase price.

It's a kind of give-and-take. You give something up to get something you want. You give up the idea of getting a ready-to-go, polished home and settle for a fixer. In exchange, you get to live in the neighborhood you want.

Will You Like It Because It's Just Plain Fun?

I believe that almost everyone is a handyman at heart. Most of us like to putter around, although many of us really don't have much knowledge or experience of what to do or how to do it.

If that fits you, then working on a handyman's special can be one of the great experiences of your life (assuming you also take to heart the lessons in this book). If you are already handy and experienced, I shouldn't have to say more. You already know the excitement of starting a new hands-on project. On the other hand, if this is all new to you, but you have a hankering to try, then there's no better way to learn than by doing. Buying a fixer lets you jump in with both feet and, as long as you go slowly, lets you learn and succeed as you go.

I've had some of the best times of my life fixing up houses with my wife. I suspect the same could hold true for you. (Check the quiz at the end of this chapter to see if you're the sort of person who would do well with a handyman's special.)

I'm assuming that by now you have a pretty good idea of what a fixer is. (You'll learn all about the four types of fixers in the next chapter.) It should be clear that what we're talking about is a house with a problem. It could be anything from needing a good coat of paint to being cracked in half because of a hurricane. A fixer is really a property in anything less than perfect condition.

So, why do YOU want such a property? Or do you?

Take this short quiz to help you determine if you really do want a fixer-upper.

*D*o You Want a Fixer-Upper?

1. Do you have a lot of spare time?

2. Are you willing to work with your hands to make money (as opposed to just working with your mind)?

3. Are you unable to afford a house in the neighborhood of your dreams?

4. Do you think in terms of "profit" instead of in terms of "salary"?

5. Are you willing to live in a home that's permanently "under construction"?

6. Are you a "handy" person?

7. If necessary, will your "significant other" be willing to work at a regular job (to provide a steady income, health benefits and so forth) while you work on a property?

8. Are you willing to spend a lot of time looking and then getting "down and dirty" in making low-ball offers and creative real estate deals?

9. Does the whole idea of taking on a handyman's special sound like fun to you?

10. Are you a risk taker?

Obviously, this informal quiz isn't going to finally determine whether or not you'd do well tackling a fixer. On the other hand, the more "yes" answers you gave, the more likely you're the sort who's already out there looking for those properties that look bad—and profitable—instead of those that look good.

Answers:

Yes to all 10: Give yourself the golden hammer award!

7–9: You're probably a do-it-yourselfer who needs a bigger project.

5–6: You like the money-making angle, but are wary of the work.

1–4: Have you considered stocks and bonds?

CHAPTER 2

Is It a True Fixer?

How do you know a fixer when you see one?

We all rely heavily on first impressions. But first impressions can sometimes be very wrong. For example, if the toilets and sinks are ripped out, there are big holes in the walls and the windows are all broken, most of us would concede that we were looking at a fixer.

On the other hand, what if the property looks to be in prime shape, virtually a model home? Would we automatically conclude that there were no fixer opportunities here? If we did, we might be mistaken. The good-looking property could still be a fixer because of hidden problems that have been covered over. The second home could require more work than the obviously bad-looking property, which probably needs only cosmetic work to put it back into good shape. Indeed, sometimes the worst looking fixers are the easiest to handle, while those that look good aren't really showing their true problems. (This is a big reason that wise buyers today insist on home inspections!)

The truth is that fixers not only come in all shapes and sizes, but also in all conditions of damage. All of which brings us to what a fixer really is. How run-down does a property have to be to be considered a fixer? How can you tell the true condition? And when is it time to simply shake your head and say that the building is too far gone and should just be demolished?

These are important questions. How you answer them will determine if you're successful at finding, buying and fixing up properties. It will also determine how good a fit the property you find is when compared to your level of skill at fixing it up. (If you don't accurately identify the type of fixer you are looking at, how do you know you won't buy a property that's too difficult for you to handle?)

To help you recognize the types of fixers, here are the four main categories. We'll consider each separately.

---

*T*ypes of Fixer-Uppers

1. Cosmetic

2. Rejuvenator

3. Broken-Back

4. Scraper

What Is a Cosmetic Fixer?

If you've spent any time at all looking at homes, you'll know this type when you see it. Basically, there's nothing wrong with the structure—it just looks bad. Typically, the paint will be old, stained, dirty or even peeling. Windows may be cracked. Sinks may be broken or missing. The carpet may be stained or torn. The yard is totally run-down, the lawn and shrubbery dead or dying.

This is the perfect fixer for most people. The worse the place looks, the better. You *want* the front door to be hanging at an angle on broken hinges. You want there to be holes in the walls. You want the light fixtures to have been stolen with just bare wires hanging from the ceilings.

Why do you want this? Because the worse the place looks, the more difficult it is for the seller to find a buyer and the lower the price will have to be.

Keep two things in mind: First, most sellers who have this kind of property realize what the problem is and spend a few thousand dollars making it look better. They can have the whole inside and outside spray painted, some cheap carpeting put in, fixtures replaced and in a few weeks get tens of thousands more for the better-looking home. But not all sellers are savvy, some don't have the money and some just don't care. These will put the house up for sale as is (or let it go to foreclosure, which we'll cover in a later chapter). In short, while they aren't usually available in abundance in good neighborhoods, these properties are around if you look thoroughly.

The second thing to keep in mind is that as bad as the description I've given of this property is, *everything* I've noted is still cosmetic. By this I mean, you can fix it all with paint, plaster, carpeting and some new fixtures. You or I or any handyperson can do it. You don't need the services of a professional plumber or electrician. It's easily doable. All that's needed is a little time, a little money and some design skills (picking colors, textures and so on).

What Is a Rejuvenator?

The next type of fixer is a bit different. While it may sometimes look much the same as the cosmetic fixer, most of the time it looks better. Often it's not run-down very much and it may need relatively little paint, plaster and superficial repair work. What it does need, however, is some basic upgrading that may not show.

The typical rejuvenator is an older home. And because it's older, it's obsolete. It may lack insulation and an adequate heating system (by modern standards). The plumbing may leak and be clogged, or the wiring may not handle modern loads (such as required by a clothes washer, dryer and big refrigerator). Maybe the home has wood floors that have been infested with termites and require removal and replacement. Or perhaps the house is so old-fashioned that it has an outhouse instead of a bathroom. (Don't laugh! Sometimes these "quaint" old places coexist for long periods of time with modern homes before they are discovered by people such as yourself.)

In short, time has simply passed by this type of home.

The problem with the rejuventor is that it's in far worse shape than it looks. Often the owner will turn a deaf ear to arguments that the house needs tens of thousands of dollars in updating that really doesn't show. Instead, the owner may try to sell it for what modern homes in the neighborhood are going for. Indeed, occasionally an unwary buyer, thinking it's just a cosmetic fixer, may wander in and purchase this home for far more than it's worth.

Usually, however, most people who come by do realize the problems (especially today, with home inspections and seller disclosures becoming the rule). And the house just sits there, aging, so to speak. If you're lucky, you'll find this home after it's been on the market for a year or so, and you'll be able to get the seller to accept a realistic offer. But, then be prepared for not only hard labor, but also work that may require the skills (along with commensurate expense) of professionals.

What Is a Broken-Back Fixer?

This type of fixer can be old or new, cosmetically clean or a rat's nest, rejuvenated or decrepit. What sets it apart is that it has an apparently implacable problem.

What could such a problem be? The broken-back fixer may only have one bathroom and two bedrooms where the minimum acceptable for the neighborhood is two bathrooms and three bedrooms. (Often in this case, a former owner may have tried to add on an extra bathroom and bedroom, only making the place worse by bad workmanship.)

Or, the place could have a seriously cracked foundation. Or it could be on a hillside where the ground is shifting and threatening to destroy the house. Or the seller may have tried to put on a new and far heavier roof, only to have the roof beams collapse. Or there could be earthquake, hurricane, tornado or other damage. I've seen all of these and I'm sure there are dozens more problems I haven't mentioned.

In short, the house has a big problem that looks impossible to fix. Hence, the seller, realizing the difficulty, is willing to let the place go for a fraction of its value were it fixed up. (Or the bank has repossessed and the lender is trying to dump the dog.)

The key to successfully handling the broken-back fixer is to come up with a creative way of correcting the problem that works, that isn't difficult to do and that doesn't cost a lot of money. Some very creative people have made fortunes doing nothing but going around and solving apparently unsolvable problems with this type of fixer home.

What Is a Scraper?

Finally, we come to the ultimate fixer, a house with no future. I once owned just such a place. It was on a valuable lot, but the home had been built at the turn of the century and didn't have a cement foundation. Instead, it used an older "mudsill" method. It didn't have conventional walls, which are essentially made of a framework onto which an outside and interior sheeting is nailed. It just had slats nailed diagonally together to make the walls. The bathroom was on the back porch. The plumbing was primitive. The electrical system was dangerous. The roof was made of a wild hodge-podge of shingles, tin and tar paper. I think you get the idea. It was beyond having an "implacable problem." It was hopeless.

What to do?

With a "scraper," the key is to buy the property very cheaply because of the obvious problem with the house. You buy it so cheaply, in fact, that you can afford to "scrape" it off the lot and start from scratch building a new home.

What would be the advantage here over, say, simply buying an already built new home or an already empty lot? One advantage is neighborhood. Often these scrapers are in dynamite neighborhoods where there are no more available lots. You can buy the property cheaply, quickly put up a house and sell for a ton of money. It's being done every day in almost every good, older neighborhood around the country.

Also, these homes are usually already connected to sewer and utilities, and since you are "renovating" instead of starting with a virgin lot, it may be a lot simpler to get city and county permits as well as get permissions through the building and planning department.

The key here, as noted, is to get the lot cheap enough. However, that's often as big a problem as with the other types of fixers because the seller often sees not just the lot, but the lot and the house that's currently on it. (Such sellers refuse to see the existing house as a liability—that is, it will cost money to have it scraped off—and instead insist that the house is really an asset.)

But, you come in, convince the seller to be realistic, put up a finer, bigger and more lush house (though being careful not to overbuild for the neighborhood), and thus dramatically increase the property's value. In the end, you sell for a profit.

These are the four types of handyman's specials you're likely to encounter. We'll have more to say about each of them as we go through this book. But for now, ask yourself which level you can handle.

What Type of Work Can You Do?

Each of the four fixer types just mentioned will require specific kinds of work. If you're like most who purchase these properties, you'll plan to do much of the work yourself. (We'll have more to say about hiring out jobs in Chapter 11.) After all, one sure way to save money is to do the labor on your own.

At the outset, it's important to understand your own level of skill. What kind of work and how much are you willing to do yourself? What kind of work do you feel is too difficult for you?

It's also important that the type of fixer you buy be a good match for the level of work you want to do. The worst thing that can happen is for you to buy a fixer only to discover that it requires work that's simply too much for you. In this situation, you might have to hire expensive professionals not only to do the actual labor, but also to do the design and planning as well. This could turn an otherwise potentially profitable fixer into a money pit.

Therefore, at the onset, "know thyself."

Rule

Don't overestimate . . . or underestimate your abilities.

To help you judge, here are some clues as to what you might be able to handle given the level of job you'll feel comfortable with.

Are You a "Dabbler"?

My wife is this type of personality when it comes to handyman's specials. She actually enjoys doing painting and wallpapering, tasks which I find tedious. And though she might not enjoy it, she's willing to do cleaning if necessary. (You can hire a crew to come in for a day to make an entire house almost spotless for about $200.) However, my wife won't touch anything that requires even the simplest electrical or plumbing work. Things such as putting in a new wall switch, installing a new garbage disposal or hanging a new light fixture, she leaves to a handyman (me).

Between the two of us, at this level, we are essentially dabblers. We are always on the lookout for another fixer house, but my wife looks primarily at the cosmetics of the place. She understands her limitations and, were it not for me, would never consider any property other than a cosmetic fixer.

If you're a dabbler, be aware that there are plenty of properties out there waiting for you. You will be able to buy them at discount and, by doing the work largely by yourself, you should be able to resell at a profit. Probably not for as big a profit as if you had taken on some of the other types of fixers. But, then again, you won't have strained your pocketbook, your back or your psyche.

Are You an "Enthusiast"?

I'm probably in this category, although I've taken on all kinds of fixer projects in my time. I like to look at the house's systems. If there's a heating system that needs work, I'll try to figure out how to best fix it. If the house needs to be completely replumbed, I feel confident I can do it.

In more serious cases, I also like the creativity involved in solving an apparently unsolvable problem. I've worked on houses that were slipping down hillsides (installing new foundations to hold them in place), taken on cracked foundations and slabs (stabilizing these in many different ways), tackled broken roofs and so on. For me, these tasks are actually fun! I enjoy the challenge of first figuring out a solution and then trying it to see if it really works.

For me, as for other enthusiasts, the middle two types of fixers are ideal; that is, the "rejuvenator" and the "broken-back." I don't see these as threats, but as opportunities. In fact, I can hardly wait to get started with plans and the actual work. As noted, I'm willing to do a simpler cosmetic fixer, because that's what my wife prefers. But, the more serious problems are *my* cup of tea.

Are You a "Builder"?

Finally, we come to the "builder." This person often is, indeed, in the building trades and does have a contractor's license (although that's not normally necessary for working on your own home). The builder likes to do the job right; that is, from the ground up. This sort of person typically doesn't enjoy going back and remodeling or fixing up. What the builders wants to do is design a home or other property from scratch. Builders want to do the foundation, the walls, the roof, the ceilings—everything.

But, unlike major contractors, they usually don't want to do it full-time. They prefer it be an *avocation* rather than a vocation. As a result, the "scraper" is ideal for them.

Yes, they may take on the other types (though rarely just the cosmetic fixers), but they won't be happy unless they're doing the real thing.

I've done a few buildings from the ground up and, yes, it can be very satisfying to sit back and look at the building that you've created. But, I don't personally find the tasks of scheduling, working with material suppliers and subcontractors, fighting "city hall" over plans, and all the other problems associated with building from scratch to be enjoyable. But, I have no quarrel with those that do. If you fit this mold, then by all means go with what you do best. Besides, you're the sort whose most likely to make the most money in the field.

How Do You Get the Right Mix?

Here, then, are the four types of houses and the three types of people who get into fixing up. I've positioned them in their most likely match-ups. Do you know where you fit in? (If you're not sure, take the quiz at the end of this chapter.)

What's Your Fixing-Up Comfort Level?

As noted, for most of us the level of comfort with fixing up is the first, the dabbler. We can easily handle painting and

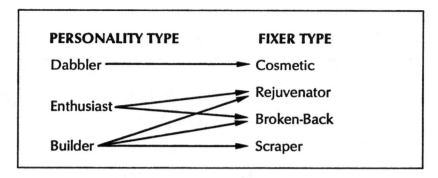

wallpapering. We can replace fixtures and do basic plumbing and electrical work. But, we really don't want to tackle much more.

At the other extreme is the builder who is confident and capable of scraping a lot and starting from scratch.

And in between is the enthusiast who is willing to tackle big jobs in older houses or work creatively to solve an apparently unsolvable problem.

To help you determine what category you fall into, take the following quiz. No one has to see your answers. (There are no right or wrong answers.) It may help you to get a better sense of just what level of fixer you can handle.

*W*hat Level of Fixer Can You Handle?

1. Do you enjoy painting and wallpapering?

2. What about hammering, sawing and assembling?

3. Do you feel comfortable changing a wall switch?

4. Have you ever installed a sink, toilet or shower?

5. Do you know how (or do you feel sure you can learn how) to remove a glass frame in order to get a broken window repaired?

6. Do you feel comfortable walking on a roof looking for leaks?

7. Can you plant a garden including lawn and shrubs?

8. Would you have no trouble patching and then painting the entire exterior of a home?

9. If a chimney were missing a few bricks, could you cement them back in place?

10. If a backyard fence had fallen over, could you sink new posts and fix the fence?

11. Are you willing to quit your regular job (while your spouse continues to work) and risk your money on a fixer?

12. Are you able to lay tile on a kitchen counter as well as install a new sink?

13. Have you ever installed (or helped install) a furnace? A water heater? A whole house air conditioner?

14. If you were in the attic, would you recognize a ground wire? Would you know if the ground wire were missing?

15. Could you install and populate a 200-amp circuit breaker box?

16. Could you work with engineers, concrete pourers, steel welders and others to come up with a plan for stabilizing a broken foundation?

17. Would you feel comfortable installing duct work for a furnace/air conditioner?

18. Could you get building plans, push them through building and planning departments, hire subcontractors and workers, supervise work, handle problems as they appeared and complete a new building project?

19. Are you capable of going to a lender and getting financing for a project that's only on paper?

20. Do you know what a sofit, "cripple" and dormer are? (A sofit is the underside of a stairway or overhang. A "cripple" is a short weaker wall. A dormer is a window sticking out perpendicular to a roof. If you had to read here to figure these out, mark "no.")

About Your Answers

Obviously the more times you answer "yes," the more experience and knowledge you have with fixers. However, just because you can't answer yes to all questions doesn't mean that you can't do all types of properties from cosmetic fixers to scrapers. It may mean, however, that you will need more time on the learning curve.

All of which is to say, just take this test with a big grain of salt. It doesn't "prove" anything about your ability to succeed. But, it may show quite a bit about your current level of experience and, hence, the type of handyman's special personality you are right now.

Scoring

All 20: You're definitely a builder. You can tackle any project. But be careful about becoming involved in cosmetic fixers that are too easy, lest you quickly get bored.

15–19: Pretty darn good. You're definitely enthusiastic about this field and, I suspect, have had some success in it along the way. You, too, could tackle just about anything, but be wary of those scrapers. You could get in over your head.

10–14: You're also an enthusiast and are probably quite handy. While a cosmetic fixer would be easily within your grasp, a rejuvenator or a broken-back fixer would definitely be a challenge.

5–9: Temper your enthusiasm with a touch of reality. Thus far, you're probably only a dabbler. A cosmetic fixer would suit you very well, while more challenging fixers might be a bit too much just yet.

0–4: There's also room for those who sit on the sidelines and cheer. Why not take a course at a local school to learn some important skills before plunging into the handyman's special business?

CHAPTER 3

Where You Can Find a Good Fixer

Fixers occur in almost every neighborhood in every county and state. However, there are some areas where you are more likely to find them and some better ways of looking for them than others.

Have You Considered Older Areas?

The age of a neighborhood is a definite factor in determining whether and how many fixers will be in it.

Most cities in the United States have developed outward from a central core. First came the original development, perhaps at the turn of the century or earlier. Then came the suburbs, often spreading out during the 1940s, 1950s and 1960s. And then, more recently, came the far suburbs located miles from the old central city and often containing complete

---

Hint

Older areas, particularly those that have aged well and are still popular, are happy hunting ground for fixers.

---

shopping and other facilities themselves—sort of like self-contained villages.

If you were to graphically plot the typical American city, it might look something like Figure 3.1.

Have You Looked in the Central Core?

The most ideal place to find a fixer is in an area of the central core that has not been blighted. Too many city centers have been abandoned and left to run down. House after house is in ruin. This is not an opportunity for a person looking for a fixer; it is a challenge for government to revitalize and remake.

However, in many central core areas, there are large pockets of older homes, often well constructed on big lots, that have retained their elegance. These fashionable older neighborhoods typically have modest crime rates, are ethnically mixed and offer charming buildings. While the prices may still be fairly high, they often are not as high as the most popular suburbs. Most important of all, there are usually lots of fixers.

You won't have trouble identifying these areas. You can immediately see that the buildings are all older. Further, just drive down any street and you'll immediately see that the vast majority of homes are well kept, with lawns and shrubs manicured and houses having new coats of paint. (Some areas

FIGURE 3.1

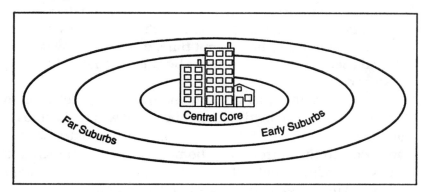

have been taken back from urban blight and rejuvenated by a combination of government and public effort.) Of course, in every block there will be one or two that stand out because the yard is a mess and the house looks dilapidated. You've just found a fixer! By the way, all kinds of fixers should be available here, from cosmetic to scrapers.

What About the Early Suburbs?

This is where most people look. However, it's not the best place to find *good* fixers. The early suburbs are now the aging suburbs. The homes built there are now reaching the end of their life span of 40 to 50 years. Also consider that older suburbs in many areas are now rapidly becoming the new slums.

As a result, there are often many fixers in the early suburbs. However, the very fact that there are so many often works against them. A very important rule of real estate is to remember that while you can do wonders for an individual property, by yourself you can't help a neighborhood. There's nothing worse than to buy a house, put time, money and sweat into against them. A very important rule of real estate is to remember that while you can do wonders for an individual property, by yourself you can't help a neighborhood. There's nothing worse than to buy a house, put time, money and sweat into it, and then not be able to resell because the neighborhood is so bad.

My suggestion is that if you're interested in purchasing in an early suburb (defined as a neighborhood where the houses are between 25 and 50 years old), you pay extra special attention to the surrounding homes. Check out the area in the surrounding blocks. If the houses have been largely kept up, if lawns and gardens look good, if there's a sense of well-being and security, then you've found a pocket where buying a fixer can make great sense.

On the other hand, if the yards are run-down, the houses neglected and there's a feeling of danger and crime in the area, you'd be wasting your money trying to fix up such a place.

---

*R*ule

No matter how much money, time and effort you spend (and sometimes you can spend too much), you can never overcome a bad neighborhood.

You're going to find mostly a lot of cosmetic fixers in the early suburbs. There will also be some rejuvenators and broken-backs, but you're not likely to find any scrapers.

Do You Want the Far Suburbs?

Since the early 1970s, people leaving the central city have moved even farther to what I call the far suburbs. These are such great driving distances from the city (sometimes 20 miles or more, particularly in the western states) that they are almost, but not quite, their own cities.

These far suburbs contain the newer homes and, often, the most upscale neighborhoods. Sometimes they have gated communities. Usually the streets are wide and greenbelts and walking trails are not uncommon. They are often low crime areas and are usually considered the most desirable neighborhoods by those who don't mind a long trek to work either driving or on the train.

A fixer in such a neighborhood is also highly desirable because of the quick and strong resale potential. These are the areas where you are most likely to be able to turn around a property in a very short time.

However, you're not likely to find all types of fixers here. Typically you'll find two types of fixers. One will be the cosmetic fixer, often associated with a foreclosure or an REO sale (discussed shortly).

The other kind you're likely to find is a broken-back fixer. Here, although the house is relatively new, some problem usually not handled well during construction is causing the difficulty. In California, for example, you will often find fixers in those neighborhoods that have problems with hills sliding, mainly because the houses were not properly secured when they were built. There are enthusiasts who make a good living going around, finding these properties and correcting the problems using creative techniques. In other areas of the country, sinking ground, construction not suitable for the climate or the weather (wind, storms, etc.) create similar opportunities.

Will You Consider Mixed Types of Housing?

Thus far, we've been looking at the location of neighborhoods. Now, however, let's concentrate on the types of housing found within a neighborhood. There are two general groups. Either the home will be in a tract, in which case all the other homes are similar, or it will be in a custom area, in which eclecticism rules and you have a wide variety of styles.

Given the choice of getting a fixer in a tract or in a custom area (all else being equal), go with the custom area every time. The reason is potential.

In a tract area, you can never do more to a house than bring it back to its former state. The reason is simple: there are too many comparables. In real estate, value is determined by what similar properties recently sold for. The house you have, in a tract, is likely to have a dozen comparables that sold over the last year. As a result, its price is locked. Everything you do to the place to make it better than its cousins will be considered "overfixing." The result is you won't get your money out.

Don't think that value is based on how much money you spend fixing up a place, or how much time and effort you spend working on it. Remember, no one wants to get stuck with an overbuilt white elephant.

---

*R*ule

The value of a property is what someone will pay you when you try to resell . . . and buyers won't pay much more than what comparables sold for.

On the other hand, this rule goes out the window in a custom area. Here you may have a house of 1,500 square feet next to one of 3,000 square feet. You will have all types of architectural designs, lot sizes and even landscaping.

As a result, fixing your selling price becomes more difficult. Appraisers, who are hard pressed in custom areas, will often look for comparables on the basis of square footage or location.

In short, you have the opportunity here to be more creative with what and how you fix up, and at the same time still have the good hope of being able to get your money out and realize a profit.

Are There Opportunities in REOs?

REO stands for "Real Estate Owned." It refers to property that a lender, such as a bank or savings and loan, has taken back through foreclosure. Now the lender owns it instead of an individual. And, the lender who is in the business of making loans and not owning property wants to get rid of it as soon as possible.

REOs are almost always fixers. The reason why is actually quite simple. If you were going to lose your house to the bank through foreclosure, would you spend a lot of time keeping it in good shape, or would you just let it run down? Further, there's often a lot of anger on the part of borrowers who are losing their homes. Hence, houses that are taken back will often have moderate-to-severe damage, including holes in walls, broken windows, broken toilets and sinks, damaged heaters and air conditioners and so on. Of course, as we've learned in the last chapter, this is really all cosmetic damage.

Lenders, however, are not stupid (no matter how crazy their lending policies may seem; see a later chapter on finance), and they will make a decision with an REO to either fix it up themselves (in which case it's no longer of interest to us) or to sell it "as is" (in which case we're very much interested).

In areas where the housing market is still depressed after the housing recession of the early 1990s, there are often a great many REOs that need fixing up. Indeed, there are often so many that lenders give up on trying to fix them up themselves and sell them all "as is" hoping to dump as many as quickly as possible. (Too many REOs on the books and the government will close a lender down.)

Is an REO a Bargain?

This provides opportunities. While the rules for neighborhoods discussed above don't change, the chances for finding a good fixer increase. However, keep in mind that lenders are tough negotiators. You may come in with a low-ball offer (discussed in the next section) and be unable to pin a lender down. The lender may simply stall, hoping to get a better offer.

Since they are in the business, lenders know pretty closely what a house is worth in any given condition and they're always trying to shave a little higher price for themselves. The great danger, therefore, is that because it's an REO you may think it's a better deal than it really is.

A few years ago I bought an REO that was in terrible condition. I got it for about a third less than market price for a similar home in good shape and thought I had done well. But, by the time I fixed up all the problems it had and resold it, I barely got my investment in time and money back, let alone made a profit. It was an expensive lesson to learn.

REOs may offer a great opportunity. Or, they may simply be a glitzy, overpriced fixer. Be careful and take a *long* look before you buy one.

Government REOs

In many areas of the country the government, through its FHA or Veterans programs, will offer REOs for sale. These are homes taken back through foreclosure by lenders and then assumed by a government agency as part of its insurance or guarantee to the lender. Almost without exception, these homes are in terrible shape. Some the government will fix up before offering for sale. Forget about these. Although the prices asked are often slightly below market, these homes do not offer a fix-up opportunity.

Others, however, the government will offer "as is." I've found these to be real opportunities in some cases. Although the damage is usually cosmetic (as we've defined it here), the prices are often rock bottom. If there are no or few other bidders, you can sometimes really get a steal here.

But, again, be careful. The temptation to overpay because it's an REO always is there.

Can You Find a Foreclosure?

Foreclosure is the process a lender goes through to take back a home from a borrower who hasn't made the mortgage payments. The time required for the process itself varies by state from only a few months to as much as a year. Until title to the property has transferred back to the lender (and it becomes an REO), however, it is still owned by the borrower. And the borrowers are almost always desperately trying to sell to get out from under the foreclosure.

While in today's market many foreclosure sales are caused by the borrower being financially upside down (owing more than the house is worth), sometimes there are other reasons. The borrower could simply be a bad manager of money, or have lost jobs, gotten sick, be required to move to a new job or have any number of other reasons.

Usually, during the early days of the foreclosure process, the borrower will keep up the property when there's high hopes of getting a quick sale. But, as the grim reaper draws closer, typically the borrower lets things run down. Sometimes a foreclosure will take a year or longer to conclude and a property can deteriorate during that time into terrible shape.

As a result, there are many handyman's special opportunities in foreclosures. Again, the same rules of neighborhoods apply. However, there are some important caveats here.

Added Risk

When you're dealing with a seller in foreclosure, you run the risk of that seller coming back at a later time and claiming that you used undue influence to get a lower than necessary price. (This is only a danger if property values subsequently go higher.) Some states allow sellers in such predicaments to reclaim their property. Check with an attorney in your area.

Further, you must deal not only with the seller, but with the lender. The lender will always add in back payments including interest and penalties. As a consequence, the price to get the house out of foreclosure and purchase it may be higher than the seller realizes. You may end up wasting a lot of time thinking you could buy at one price, only to find that the actual price is much higher, too high for you to buy, fix up and make a profit.

***

*C*aution

_____

The seller of a house in foreclosure may have a long-term right of redemption.

***

Added Opportunity

On the other hand, you may have leverage with the lender. Particularly in a bad real estate market where there are a lot of foreclosures, you may be able to work out a deal whereby the lender forgoes certain interest amounts and penalties, sometimes even principal, in order to get rid of the mortgage.

Of course, no lender is going to come to you with such an offer. It's the sort of thing you must negotiate yourself. If you find yourself in such a position, I suggest you read my book *Tips & Traps for Negotiating Better Real Estate Deals* (McGraw-Hill, 1995).

What Are the Sources of Fixers?

Just knowing that you're in the right neighborhood, that there might be REOs or foreclosures around, isn't quite enough, however. You have to make the actual contact. You have to find the actual handyman's special house. How do you do that?

Those who are experienced in the field know that it's mostly a matter of keeping your feelers out. You have to let people know you're looking and spend some time gathering information.

For example, when I'm looking for a fixer, I usually begin by defining an area, a particular neighborhood or group of neighborhoods. Then I do the following:

Check Advertising

I read all the local papers that advertise property for sale, including throwaways and weeklies. (You never know where someone will advertise.)

Check Bulletin Boards

I always stop at all the local grocery stores and pharmacies to check out their bulletin boards. A desperate seller will often pin a 3" × 5" card asking for buyers.

Drive the Neighborhoods

I also drive all the streets in the neighborhood(s) I'm interested in as often as possible. I look for FSBO (For Sale by Owner) signs as well as obviously run-down properties. I call the FSBOs and find out if there's a fixer opportunity. I leave a business card (or note) on the run-down houses asking the owners to contact me if they want to sell. (You'd be surprised how often I get a call back!)

Talk to Brokers

Of course, I also always talk to brokers in the area. Brokers list 90 percent or more of properties for sale in most areas. I tell them what I want and they try to oblige by finding me the right house.

Keep in mind, however, that not all agents "cobroke" properties. That is, they don't cooperate on the sale of every house with all other brokers. Some they handle themselves. This is particularly the case with houses that they think they can sell quickly. Sometimes a fixer in a good neighborhood is just such a house.

What this means is that you need to talk to more than one broker. I suggest you work with a broker for, say, a week or two, and look at the houses available then. When you've exhausted that supply and still haven't seen anything you like, let the broker know you're still looking and to give you a call if anything that fits the bill shows up.

Then contact other brokers. Explain what you've seen and ask if they have anything else. They may very well have just what you're looking for!

Using this strategy, you should fairly quickly be able to see nearly all of the houses listed on the market in an area and hopefully one of those will be just right for you.

Note: We'll cover determining how much to offer and making a bid on a house in the next section in this book.

Other Property Types

Thus far we've been discussing homes almost exclusively. However, there are other types of fixers. For example, if you're looking for a bigger challenge you may want to buy a fixer apartment building, industrial building or even a small commercial strip. Many times these other property types offer greater opportunities than homes.

Apartment Buildings

I've tackled this type of fixer and I can assure you it's a real challenge. Whatever you would do in a house, you have to do many times over. The problems escalate as the number of units increase. Even a small four-unit building (fourplex) can be a full-time job when it comes to fixing up. After all, you have to fix up four times as many kitchens, baths, bedrooms, etc. On the other hand, when you're done, you tend to make four times as much money.

Run-down apartment buildings are becoming a real opportunity as real estate pulls out of its recent recession. Many of these simply couldn't be sold before and the owners let them go. Now, for the right person, the opportunity exists for moving in, fixing up, renting out and reselling.

What Should You Watch Out For?

- Dangerous Neighborhoods—Don't buy in an area where you'd be afraid to go at night to collect the rent.

- Structural Problems—With a house, it's only one unit that's empty. With an apartment building, you could be losing rent on all units while the structure is being fixed. (There are dozens of apartment buildings in good areas of the San Fernando Valley near Los Angeles that are structurally damaged because of the 1994 earthquake. They can't be rented out until they're fixed and they can't be fixed because the owners don't have the cash from rent. They're not an opportunity, but a trap.)

- Low Occupancy Areas—Remember, an apartment building is a business. If there aren't enough tenants around to fill it, regardless of how good a fixer candidate it is, you'll eventually go out of business.

Industrial Buildings

There are relatively few fixer opportunities here, simply because in most cases the structure is just a shell with the tenant making improvements. However, occasionally a whole industrial area will be run down with no tenants.

The key to success is to find the kind of tenant who wants this building, then fix it up just to suit the tenant. An example is taking a large industrial building and converting it into many small office suites where there's a need for office space, but little need for industrial usage.

Commercial Strip Center

Usually opportunities here come about because the individuals who own them have let these properties run down to the point where they can't get high-paying commercial tenants. Because the price is based on the income, you can often get these run-down strip centers for a song.

The trick is to fix them up to the point where a strong tenant will want to move in. Once you have one strong tenant, others will follow and eventually you'll have high rents and be able to sell for a profit.

Condos and Co-ops

Finally, it's important to say a word or two about fixing up condos and co-ops. Generally speaking, the only type of condo/co-op fixer you should consider is a cosmetic one. If you think about it for a moment, it should become clear as to why.

When you purchase a shared ownership type of property, the only part of the house that you really control is inside your living area. The roof, outside walls, foundation, structure and so on are all owned in common and administered through the homeowners' association (HOA). Therefore, any damage problems must be handled through the HOA.

As a result, you won't find many condos/co-ops with serious problems. At most they'll need paint, cleanups and fixture repair/replacement. While this can knock the price down a bit, it's unlikely to cause those deep price discounts that you'll find in the other types of fixers.

In this chapter we've looked at where you're likely to find a good handyman's special. Now let's turn our attention to evaluating a fixer to determine how much it's truly worth.

*C*hecklist for Finding a Good Fixer

Yes	No		
❑	❑	1.	If your fixer is in a central city area, is it in a good pocket neighborhood?
❑	❑	2.	If you're in an early suburb, have you checked to see that the neighborhood isn't on the way down?
❑	❑	3.	If you're in a far suburb, have you checked to see if the property has a serious flaw?
❑	❑	4.	Have you selected a custom house over a tract home?
❑	❑	5.	If it's a tract home, are you comfortable with the reduced profit potential?
❑	❑	6.	If you're looking at an REO, are you treating it like any other fixer and not paying more because it's bank owned?
❑	❑	7.	If you're dealing with a seller in foreclosure, have you called the bank and begun negotiations?
❑	❑	8.	Have you driven around in the neighborhood in which you're looking for a fixer and stopped by to talk to the owner?
❑	❑	9.	Have you contacted several brokers?
❑	❑	10.	Have you considered other types of fixer properties, such as apartment buildings or industrial and commercial buildings?

CHAPTER 4

Checking Out a Fixer Property

Let's say that you've found a handyman's special that you really like and want to buy. It's got location, it's run-down in a way you can handle and it seems like the seller is willing to talk a reasonable price. It's got everything going for it. Or does it?

Before you lay down one dollar, you need to ask some very specific questions and get some very specific answers.

Until you have a handle on the answers to the questions on the next page, there's no way you can know what a "good price" is for the property. Let's consider a fixer house that I recently almost bought.

Can You Be Saved by the Estimates?

The house was in the old part of the city in a well-preserved neighborhood. I had checked with agents and knew that

---

*W*hat You Must Know Before You Buy a Fixer

- How much work, exactly, is involved?
- How long will that work take?
- How much of that work will you do yourself?
- What will be the cost of hiring out the remainder?

---

properties were easy to sell there, mainly because of the close-in location and the nice setting.

The house I found was a two-story Victorian on Silver Avenue. (That really was the street name!) It had all kinds of gables and railings and other vintage accessories, most in pretty good shape. I had seen these houses "modernized," which is a fancy way of saying all their finery had been stripped and a cheap fiberglass roof and aluminum siding had been put on. Houses treated like this usually ended up looking ghastly. I, however, intended to restore this old place to its former grandeur, and resell for a bundle in the process.

The property was a combination cosmetic fixer and rejuvenator. It needed painting and dressing up inside and out. But it also needed a new heating/cooling system as well as electrical repairs. And I'd have to move some of the rooms around to make them more appealing for modern buyers. In short, it was a big project.

The seller, Mrs. Smith, was a little old lady who seemed to have trouble hearing and seeing (I suspected it was at least partly an act) and who kept wanting to feed me cookies and milk each time I dropped by. The house was listed, but apparently Mrs. Smith had an arrangement with her agent to show the property herself in exchange for paying a reduced commission. That was fine with me.

The asking price was $285,000, "as is." The "as is" was to let buyers know that the seller wasn't going to put up any money to fix the place. Presumably Mrs. Smith would disclose any and all problems, but it would be the buyer's task to fix them. The price, she said, was about $50,000 less than what comparable homes in first-class shape had sold for. At first glance, it seemed a handyman's special project made in heaven.

But, I knew I had to check it out. First, I verified what other comparable homes had sold for. This was fairly easy. I checked with the listing agent as well as another broker. Indeed, other properties reported to be in first-rate condition had sold during the past six months for prices ranging from $305,000 to $350,000. Mrs. Smith hadn't been fibbing about the prices.

Next, I checked out several of these comparables. I simply had my agent call the current owners of homes that had sold, explain I was planning to buy a comparable home and ask if I could come by and look at their places. Out of five calls, three agreed. Then I went by, knocked on the door and introduced myself. In all three cases, I was asked in and was shown around the house. Every house had been freshly painted and cleaned and had had its plumbing and electrical systems upgraded. In two homes, the rooms had been enlarged or combined. I had confirmed that the resale prices were indeed for fixed-up houses (as opposed to run-down places).

Next, I had to determine how much it would cost, realistically, for me to fix up the Silver Avenue house. This was a bit harder.

I made a list of the items that needed work. On the next page is what my list looked like.

When I finished my list and looked at it, I had to whistle in surprise. There was an amazing amount of work to be done.

---

*M*ajor Items To Be Fixed on Silver Avenue

Cosmetic:
- Clean yard and put in lawn and shrubs
- Replaster as needed and repaint inside
- Repaint exterior

Major Work:
- New wood roof
- New wood siding on two outside walls
- New heating system
- Upgrade plumbing system, particularly drains and bathrooms
- Upgrade electrical system

I had done many fixers by then and felt I could give a pretty accurate guesstimate for most of the items. But this was my first Victorian, so I called up several people with whom I had previously worked: an electrician, a plumber, a heating/air-conditioning person and a roofer. Because they already knew me, they agreed to come right out within the next day or two. What they told me was most revealing.

The Roof—$20,000

A proper wood roof in the original style would probably cost close to $20,000. The problem was that the old style was very labor-intensive and there were only a few roofers who could do that kind of work. My roofer friend could not, but recommended someone who could.

The Exterior Walls—$5,000

The house had originally used clapboard on the outside. Much of it appeared to be the original. Replacing it wouldn't be difficult, but would require peeling the old rotted boards away and then replacing them with new boards. My estimate was $5,000.

The Heating System—$8,000

Getting forced-air heat to all of the rooms (there was currently only one old floor heater in the living room downstairs) would require cutting through floors and walls and would be prohibitively expensive. The less expensive way to go was individual electric wallboard heaters in each room. The problem with these was that they were very costly to operate and most buyers realized this. Installing them would cut back on the resaleability of the home. I decided that forced air would be the way to go. The estimate was at minimum $5,000 plus the cost of rebuilding the walls and floors that had to be cut away, roughly another $3,000.

The Plumbing System—$10,000

The old plumbing system was shot. Drain pipes were corroded, broken and leaking. The fresh-water pipes were old galvanized steel and were corroded with red rust marks in countless places. The house would have to be replumbed with copper. To replumb this two-story house, the cost would be about $10,000.

The Electrical System—$10,000

The house had originally been outfitted for gas lighting. Sometime in the 1920s, the owner had added old-fashioned, two-strand wiring, the kind where the thinly insulated wires are held about an inch apart by insulators placed every few feet. It was a building inspector's nightmare. The house would have to be rewired with a new circuit breaker box installed. Because it was retrofitting and meant cutting into walls, ceilings and floors, again it was more expensive. The estimate was $10,000.

Clean-Up, Replastering and Painting—$5,000

I just put down a guess for this at $5,000.

Note: In many cases I would be doing the work myself. However, when estimating costs, I always put down what it would cost as if I hired it out. That way, in case I do have to hire out, I'm not going to lose money. And if I, in fact, do it myself, I'm paying me a reasonable salary for work performed.

My Estimate of Purchase and Resale Costs

To this I added both the costs of purchase and resale, which I knew from experience would total around 10 percent of the *resale price*.

$335,000 × 10%   = $33,500
Resale/Purchase Costs = $33,500

And I added to this another seven percent of the *resale price*, which I felt was the minimum profit I would expect for taking the risk of fixing up the house.

$335,000 × 7%   = $23,450
My Minimum Profit = $23,450

***M*y Estimate of Costs To Fix Up House**

Roof	$ 20,000
The Exterior Walls	5,000
The Heating System	8,000
The Plumbing System	10,000
The Electrical System	10,000
Clean-Up, Replastering and Painting	5,000
Profit	23,450
Sales Costs	33,500
Total	$114,950

Arriving at the Purchase Price

I now subtracted my total costs from what I felt I could resell the house for and came up with my offering price.

Resale Price Estimate	$335,000
Less Costs To Fix Up and Resell	−114,950
My Offer	$220,050

Note: I didn't add in the costs of interest on my mortgage during the time I was fixing up the property nor any additional interest costs on loans I would take out to pay for the fix up. The reason is that I planned on living in the property during the time I was working on it. (See Chapter 8 for more information on financing.)

Making the Offer

Much to my surprise, I found that Mrs. Smith's apparently low asking price of $285,00 was actually about $65,000 too high for me! If I paid what she wanted, I'd never be able to do the requisite work and make a profit. Indeed, I would lose a lot of money.

So, I went to Mrs. Smith and showed her my figures. I pointed out that regardless of who did the work, it would have to be done and it would cost roughly what I estimated. She could, of course, save my 7 percent profit by doing it herself, but I suggested that it might not be something she'd be willing or able to take on.

She countered by offering me cookies and milk. Then she asked me if I was trying to take advantage of an old lady. I assured her I was not, but at the same time I had no intention of letting an "old lady" take advantage of me.

We talked some more and eventually she said she would come down another $5,000 or so in price, but nothing like the amount I was offering. I thanked her for the cookies and milk, said that I simply couldn't pay more for the place, and I left.

I kept track of Mrs. Smith's house and, about four months later, she sold it for about $250,000. Subsequently I noticed that the new owners were fixing it up. I drove by occasionally, watching the work, until one day I noticed the place all boarded up. I made inquiries and found out that the new owners had not been able to keep up their mortgage payments and had abandoned the property. It was now in foreclosure.

I took a second look at the place. But the new owners had different ideas from mine. They had put on a cheap roof and started metal siding on the outside. They had made major cuts in the walls, floors and ceiling inside and the house was a mess. At that point, I saw no hope for it except as a scraper.

The Moral to Silver Avenue

I chose the Silver Avenue house specifically as the first major example in this book for an important reason. While it's easy to pick out successful fixer stories, the most important lesson to be learned in the field is when to say "no." It's better that you pass up five good deals than you buy one bad one.

Nothing will sour you faster and more permanently than overpaying for a handyman's special. You will find yourself overwhelmed by costs, work and a shrinking time line. If you don't build enough "fat" into every purchase to allow for the necessary work, to pay yourself and still make a profit, I guarantee you'll end up like the luckless buyers of Mrs. Smith's house.

Here's the one rule that you need to cut out of this book, paste over your desk and look at before you make an offer on any fixer:

Rule

NEVER, NEVER, NEVER pay more for a fixer than what you can resell it for, less ALL of your costs plus your profit.

It's a long sentence, but a simple rule. It doesn't matter if the house is located on a silver street or the seller is a little old lady who wouldn't harm a flea. Remember, it's business. If you want to be a philanthropist, that's something else. But, if you want to make money, read that rule at least once a day . . . and then follow it unswervingly.

Should You Get Expert Help?

One of the things that allowed me to quickly get estimates of the value of the property was the fact that I had a list of experts on whom I could rely. All I had to do was pull out my little black book, go down the names inside until I found a plumber, electrician and roofer, and give them a call. They were out within 24 hours. That's not the way it works if you have to call these people cold from the yellow pages of the phone book. In Chapter 5 we'll discuss putting together your own "dream team" to help you become more successful in the field.

What About "Guesstimating" Sheets?

It's very helpful to have a few "guesstimating" sheets ready for any time you check out a property. That way when you show up, you can quickly make your calculations and determine just how much you should pay.

Here are three sheets that I find indispensable (see Figures 4.1, 4.2 and 4.3).

FIGURE 4.1 The Pricing Guesstimator

Use your own expertise to take as accurate a guess as possible at what it's going to cost you to do any given fix-up job. I've just listed the more common work areas. I'm sure you'll have many more that you'll be able to add yourself:

Job	Cost Estimate	Time Required	Who'll Do It?
Fix Roof	_____	_____	_____
Fix Outside Walls	_____	_____	_____
Fix Inside Walls	_____	_____	_____
Paint Outside Walls	_____	_____	_____
Paint Inside Walls	_____	_____	_____
Landscape Yard	_____	_____	_____
Fix Heating System	_____	_____	_____
Fix Air-Conditioning	_____	_____	_____
Fix Drain Pipes	_____	_____	_____
Fix Other Plumbing	_____	_____	_____
Fix Electrical System	_____	_____	_____
Install Circuit Box	_____	_____	_____
Fix Bathroom(s)	_____	_____	_____
Fix Kitchen	_____	_____	_____
Enlarge Rooms	_____	_____	_____
Fix Foundation	_____	_____	_____
Fix Structure	_____	_____	_____
Other	_____	_____	_____

FIGURE 4.2 The Expert Advice Sheet

This covers the same ground. However, here you're no longer relying on *your* estimate, but instead have at least a verbal commitment from an expert in the field.

Job	Cost Estimate	Time Required
Fix Roof	_____	_____
Fix Outside Walls	_____	_____
Fix Inside Walls	_____	_____
Paint Outside Walls	_____	_____
Paint Inside Walls	_____	_____
Landscape Yard	_____	_____
Fix Heating System	_____	_____
Fix Air-Conditioning	_____	_____
Fix Drain Pipes	_____	_____
Fix Other Plumbing	_____	_____
Fix Electrical System	_____	_____
Install Circuit Box	_____	_____
Fix Bathroom(s)	_____	_____
Fix Kitchen	_____	_____
Enlarge Rooms	_____	_____
Fix Foundation	_____	_____
Fix Structure	_____	_____
Other	_____	_____

FIGURE 4.3 The Calculation Sheet

Here, in order to get your best offer, you're just going to fill in the blanks with the information from the other sheets, plus other information that you should already know.

Probable Resale Price*		$_____
Less Total Cost of Work To Be Done	$_____	
Less Costs of Purchase and Resale	$_____	
Less Your Profit	$_____	
Less Total Deductions		$_____
Maximum Amount To Offer		$_____

*You get this information by checking out comparable house sales in the area, those that are already fixed-up and are roughly the same location, size, number of beds/baths, quality of work and so on.

Note: If you offer more, you won't make any money. Be careful of "coming close." Some would-be fixer enthusiasts, when they get close, go back and make recalculations. This is usually a mistake. Your first calculations are based on what you think it will actually cost. Your second calculations are often based on how much you can skin off the costs in order to make the deal. Invariably, your second calculations are going to be short. With a fixer, it's better that you estimated too high in costs, than too low.

CHAPTER 5

Putting Together a "Dream Team"

Napoleon Hill, in his book *Think and Grow Rich,* was probably the first to suggest the importance of a "Master Mind" team. The idea here was to put together a group of people who had goals similar to yours, although often from different fields, with whom you could share and build ideas. They would give you support plus open your mind to new directions you hadn't considered yourself.

Napoleon Hill was a speechwriter for President Franklin Delano Roosevelt in the 1930s. Hill coined the phrase, "The only thing we need fear is fear itself" for one of Roosevelt's famous fireside chats. His book became world famous as a model for self-motivation. And although his idea for putting together a mastermind team was intended for self-motivation, we can apply the basic concept to fixing up property. What I'm talking about is putting together a "dream team" of associates who will help you find, fix up and resell properties at a much higher level than you could possibly do all by yourself. This team will work with you on projects and help you to be more successful, faster. First, however, let's consider why you need help at all. Then we'll discus putting together your dream team later in this chapter.

Do You Have an "I'll Do It Myself" Problem?

A lot of people who would be successful at fixing up homes suffer from what I call the "Renaissance Man Perspective." They feel they can do everything themselves. Just as the ultimate Renaissance man, Leonardo DaVinci, was a great painter, scientist, engineer and even a doctor, some people feel they can be a great agent, designer, financier, carpenter and so on. Whatever the task, they believe they can do it well, probably better than anyone else.

If you believe that, then you're going to spend a lot of time without receiving much in the way of rewards. Probably the greatest asset that you as a person who fixes up property can have is to know your limitations. If you've never plastered before, don't attempt to fix a plaster wall yourself–get a pro to do it. If you haven't arranged financing before, get help from an expert in the field.

Are You a "Too Determined" Do-It-Yourselfer?

It's at this point that I can hear many readers saying, "Hiring out defeats the whole purpose of getting a handyman's special. The whole point is to save money by doing it myself."

Let's consider an example that I ran into not long ago.

A good friend, Peter, bought an older home, one that I would classify as being a "broken-back" property. Its problem was that it only had one bathroom in an era where anyone

*T*wo False Presumptions

---

1. You can always do a good job by yourself.

2. Doing it yourself always saves money.

who buys a home and pays top dollar for it expects at minimum two bathrooms.

Peter's plan was to convert a closet off a second-floor master bedroom into a second bath. He did the design himself, secured the plans, ripped out the closet, hauled the tub/shower, toilet and sink upstairs, installed them, plastered the walls and did everything else on his own.

Along the way he had many delays. Because the upstairs drain wouldn't line up with the first-floor drains, he had to take out part of a ceiling and wall below. The building department repeatedly refused to pass the plumbing work that he did. He had to keep doing it over and over until finally, the inspector himself took pity and showed Peter how to do it so it would pass.

Then Peter couldn't get the tub/shower into the former closet because the doorway was too small. So he had to rip out a section of the wall. Unfortunately, it was a bearing wall and that caused the roof to sag. He not only had to repair the wall, but the roof as well. When he attached the toilet, he didn't seat it properly. It required a correctly placed wax seal, and the first time he flushed it, water gushed out all over the floor, soaking the new carpet he had put in!

Now I'm sure some people would credit Peter with his spunk and put it all down to a learning experience. However, I talked with Peter afterward and he said he had hated every minute of it. It was a frustrating experience and the only thing he said he really learned from it was to stay away from fixers.

It had taken him nearly three months to get the bathroom done. It cost him a small fortune. And the final result did not look good. It looked like the bathroom had been slapped together by an amateur, which was the truth. His work lacked the professional appearance buyers like to see, so he had trouble reselling the property.

The moral of Peter's story is that doing it by yourself, unless you are an expert in many areas, is often more costly, more time-consuming and results in poorer workmanship than to hire it out. Further, it can discourage you from working on fixers. While it's important to tackle jobs that may be a little bit harder than you're used to, it's equally important not to be overwhelmed by tasks that are nearly hopeless for you. While another person might, indeed, have had no problem doing all the work, for Peter, the task he chose for himself was simply too hard. He should have gotten expert help.

Now, I'm not suggesting that Peter should simply have called in a builder and said, "Put a bathroom there." That undoubtedly would have been even more costly. But, at critical stages along the way, he should have gotten workers who knew what they were doing to tackle the job. What were those stages?

---

*C*ritical Stages Where Expert Help Would Be a Benefit

- Design (including the kind of fixtures that would fit)

- Rough plumbing (including advice on how to install fixtures yourself)

- Plastering, carpeting, finishing—as needed

If Peter had called in experts just when he needed them, doing all the other work of which he was capable, it wouldn't have cost that much. And it would have meant getting the job done faster and better. Instead of it being a frustrating experience for him, it would have been a good learning event that would have enabled him to do even more himself the next time.

Rule

Don't be penny wise and pound foolish when it comes to fixing up. Do what you can.
But know what you can't do, and have experts do that.

How Do You Build Your Own Dream Team?

Thus far in this book we've talked about hiring experts to help you in areas where you're deficient. While this is always a good thing to do, now we're going to put a different perspective on it. Instead of "hiring," we're going to consider "participating."

Let's suppose that every Monday morning at 8:00 a.m. you met with a group of associates, all of whom were interested in doing just what you're doing: buying properties, fixing them up and ultimately selling for a profit.

Consider the make-up of this group: There might be a number of tradespeople, such as a plumber, an electrician and a roofer. But in addition, there might also be an architect, a real estate agent, a mortgage banker and an accountant/ CPA. And then there would be you, a full- or part-time entrepreneur who is devoted to successfully fixing up properties.

Consider what you all might discuss each Monday morning. The agent might say that she's seen two properties come back onto the market in the last week, either of which might be excellent choices as fixers. They were in good areas, and they were in various stages of disrepair—one a scraper and the other a rejuvenator. And the owners had tried unsuccessfully to sell them for nearly half a year, had taken them off the market and were now putting them back on at realistic prices.

Then the plumber chimed in that he had seen another property that might make an excellent fixer. He had been called in to fix a leaking water heater. But, the owners had died and the property was now in the hands of an executor who only wanted to get rid of it because it was too old, a rejuvenator, and had too many problems to rent out or sell at a good price.

Then the accountant mentioned that he had a client who had a rental she wanted to dump. The last tenants hadn't paid their rent for months, and before leaving they had trashed the place. It needed cleaning, new carpeting, some new fixtures—a true cosmetic fixer. The owner was willing to accept a very low price if she could sell quickly.

Instantly, you have four potential fixers to consider. You have the time, and so you agree to go check out each one.

You spend the next two days looking at each of them. When you call on the roofer of the group in two cases for his expert help, he's out there instantly, giving you the answers you need. You already had advice from the plumber on one property.

Eventually you narrow the field to two of the houses. Now you call on the architect for ideas on what would be best to do. Then it's the mortgage banker who quickly comes out. You tell her you've selected one property over the others and she tells you what kind of financing you could get and the best rates.

Next you call on the agent, who gets all the comparables so that you can easily see what the property should sell for, once it's fixed up. Then you check with the accountant on the tax angles. Lastly you go to see the seller and his agent to get a feeling for how amenable he would be to the kind of offer you'd like to make. The seller seems anxious enough to accept a reasonable price.

After a week, you're ready. Now, you meet again with the group and present your proposal. You describe the property, its current condition, what you would do and its potential. Those members of the group who have seen the property back you up. When you're finished, you ask who would like to participate?

The architect says he'll put in cash, in exchange for a good return on his money. The tradespeople offer their work, in exchange for a chunk of the profit when the property sells. The agent will accept a lower commission in exchange for the listing. The mortgage banker can shave a bit off the interest rate and the financing costs in exchange for financing through her. And so it goes.

By the time you're finished, you have a deal made in heaven. You have all the support you could possibly want. You have the tools to buy the property, get the job done right, and sell quickly. Further, *you* don't need to put in all the cash, all the work or all the effort.

Of course, in exchange for this, you don't get all the profit. In fact, you may only get half, or even a third of the profit. But, then again, would you have gotten such a sweet deal without your dream team?

The whole point here is that each person brings something to the table. No one member really has the time, expertise, money or enthusiasm to do it all. But, by combining the skills of the group, you create the framework around which such a project can succeed. Further, you end up doing lots and lots of fixers and everyone does very well along the way.

Do You Have the Keys To Form a Dream Team?

If I've sold you on the concept of a dream team, the next step is figuring out how to put one together. This usually requires one key person (you) who has the fire and determination to make it all work. You should always remember that around you are many, many people who are willing to participate, but who simply don't know how to get the ball rolling or are unsure of how to make things happen. Further, also remember that the participants of the dream team are not there to do anybody but themselves a favor. One way or another, they stand to benefit by the actions of the team. The agent will get a commission (or part of one) that she would not otherwise get. The tradespeople get work that they otherwise would not get. The accountant will be paid for her contribution, as will everyone else on the team in one form or another.

The whole purpose of the team, in fact, is to generate business. For you, it's the opportunity to get help in areas where you are deficient. It's also the chance to get access to properties you might otherwise miss.

So, where do you find the participants? We're going to look at how to find people to work for you in the next section. As you meet these people and work with them, if you find they are honest and eager to do more, you may want to suggest a Monday morning meeting with them. You don't need to lay the whole concept out immediately. You can just say you'd like to meet with them on a regular basis to discuss opportunities. You can do the same with your accountant, agent and others.

Expect a wide variety of reactions. Some people will be wildly enthusiastic—especially agents! Others may simply not even consider the idea and won't show up.

But, if you're persistent and make the Monday morning meeting a ritual (you're there even if only one or two other people show up), you will eventually find people climbing on board.

Also, each person you talk to knows others. Initially invite as many as possible to attend. You want to be inclusive, not exclusive. (You have plenty of time to be exclusive once your team is up and working!)

Don't overlook your social contacts. You may meet someone who's an accountant or a bricklayer at your church, your preschool or your kid's soccer game. Talk with them. Talk up the idea of a dream team, particularly if you've already set up a regular meeting time and place.

What really brings the team together is a success, and it only takes one. Find a property, use the team's resources, fix it up and sell so that everyone makes a profit. This will encourage the team to stick together for many years to come!

What "Vehicle" Should the Dream Team Use?

One of the problems with working with partners, even dream team partners, is how to formalize the relationship. It's okay to say, "When we finish, you'll get paid out of the profits," and shake hands on it. However, a lot of water can flow under the bridge between the handshake and the time the property sells and money gets distributed. It's better for all concerned to have a formal, written agreement so that they know exactly where they stand. (This is an excellent reason for having an accountant and an attorney as part of your team—they can suggest the best format and wording for your agreement.)

You may want a formal partnership agreement that's used on every deal you do. Or, it may turn out that a contract specifying the work to be performed and the distribution of profits separately for each deal works best. Decide what your team wants and what's best for each of you.

I formed my first dream team more than 30 years ago and although we have long since each gone our separate ways, I still occasionally bump into one or another of them and we reminisce about the deals we did, great and small.

Try putting together a handyman's special dream team. You will reap rich rewards if you do.

Where Do You Find Expert Help?

Before forming your dream team, you're going to need to find expert help, specialists, that you employ. (You do not *employ* dream team members.) You will often build your dream team from experts who originally worked for you. But, where do you first locate these experts?

As I've noted in earlier chapters, those who have done many fix-up jobs in the past develop a retinue of helpers they can call on. You've used Charlie to fix a roof on a house. Because he did a good job at a reasonable price, Charlie's name goes into your little black book. The next time you have a roofing problem, you call Charlie. He's worked with you before, remembers you and, hopefully, trusts you. He comes right out to give you not only a bid, but advice on the best way to get the job done.

Or you've had Linda design front yard landscaping for you. You give Linda a call and she remembers you as a good client. She pops right out and gives you a host of ideas, as well as solid cost figures, for a home you're considering buying to fix up.

Over time, by keeping track of people you use, you too will develop a little black book of names and phone numbers. Then, when you're in a spot needing either work or an estimate, you pop open your book, make a call, and the expert help you need is at hand.

How Do You Find Expert Help the First Time Out?

You can always rely on the yellow pages in the phone book. I've done that on occasion when I had no other alternative. However, the phone book usually shows dozens of names. How are you to tell who will do really good work and not charge an arm and a leg for it?

My suggestion is that you go with recommendations. Finding good expert people to help you is sort of like solving a jigsaw puzzle. As soon as you find one piece that fits, it suggests where others should go. As soon as you find one good person, he or she will suggest others who will help you.

Here are some sources you can tap when you're first looking:

1. Agents—Many real estate agents work on fixers on the side. They buy properties, clean and rebuild them, and then offer them for sale. We'll have more to say about this when we discuss the fine points of building your own dream team shortly. For now, however, remember that these agents often know and can recommend workers in many fields, including plumbing, electrical, plastering, carpentry, handyman and so on. Typically these recommendations are based on having directly worked with these people.

2. Cultivate Friends in Real Estate—The agent from whom you buy a property or who is showing you a property is usually a good source. So are the insurance

agent, the attorney you use and other people involved in deals. If he doesn't know anything about fixing up, ask if there's someone in the office who does. (There usually is.) Because you may work with several agents when you're looking for the right property, along the way you should run into several good sources. They are usually more than willing to help you out, in the hopes of getting a listing when you offer the property for resale.

3. Work with Building Inspectors—Visit your local city/ county building and ask to talk to one of the field inspectors. Chances are that if you're doing any kind of renovation work, you're going to need a permit and are going to have to deal with these people anyway.

   While these people are often very busy, I've found that if I come in late in the afternoon after they've returned from their inspections, they often don't mind chatting over a cup of coffee. Describe the kind of work you're going to be doing and ask them who does good work inexpensively in the area. These field inspectors may be able to give you some excellent leads.

4. Try Friends, Relatives, Associates—Chances are, someone you know has had some sort of work done in the not-so-distant past. Ask for a recommendation. Did the person do a good job? Did he or she charge a lot or a little? Would the person you know use that tradesperson again? But be careful with personal recommendations. Gauge who's doing the recommending. Sometimes others use far different standards from yours. Your friend Joanne may rave over someone who built custom cabinets for her. However, Joanne may be very well off and used to paying top dollar for an expert to do a job from start to finish. You, on the

other hand, may be looking for someone who's willing to do only part of the job (you'll be doing the rest) and charge cut-rate prices.

In exactly the above situation, when I was looking for a carpenter to help me fix up a kitchen, I called the custom cabinetmaker and then went over and talked to him. It quickly became obvious to both of us that I wasn't looking for the kind of work he performed. But, he was able to direct me to a carpenter/handyman who was just perfect for the job. As I said, it's like a jigsaw puzzle. Fitting in one piece leads you to seeing where others go.

5. **Check Out Advertisements**—If none of the above works for you, you will probably have to resort to looking at ads that tradespeople put out. (I consider this the weakest method because you really don't know who you're getting—you don't have the personal recommendation to rely upon.) Also check out local papers; they often have a section right at the beginning of the classifieds where tradespeople advertise. Also check out bulletin boards at supermarkets, pharmacies and elsewhere. Often tradespeople will post small ads there.

6. **Watch Out for Services**—Less helpful, from my own experience, have been services that offer to recommend local people to you for no fee. You just call up, tell them what kind of person you want and they give you a name and a number. The problem here is that these services often are financially supported by the people who are being recommended. You want to be recommended, you pay a fee, and your name goes on the list. Some services do basic screening work, but that's not always the case.

Should You Check Them Out?

No matter who you get, be sure that *you* check them out. I always ask for the names and phone numbers of at least three persons who have used the tradesperson before. Anyone who's been in the business for even six months should be able to provide you with three references.

Then I call each reference and try to determine not only what kind of work was done, but the relationship of the worker to the recommender. For example, if I'm talking to a plumber's brother-in-law, I'm less likely to put faith in the recommendation than if I'm talking to someone who is not related to the plumber!

When you make these calls, you often will rely on the words of total strangers. But, it's better than not making the calls at all. (It's surprising, but many tradespeople who give out references really don't expect you to call them and, in truth, I suspect that most people don't.)

*G*uide To Finding Expert Help and Building a *D*ream Team

1. Check with real estate agents for recommendations.

2. Call your local building inspector for referrals.

3. Check with friends, relatives and associates for recommendations.

4. Check out advertisements in the papers, bulletin boards and elsewhere.

5. Call all references.

6. Begin having dream team meetings on a regular basis and invite tradespeople with whom you've worked.

7. Talk up your dream team idea at social gatherings, at work and wherever you find a receptive audience. Ask people to attend your meetings.

8. Strive to diversify. You don't need seven agents and one carpenter. Once you've got someone who fills a particular need, look for people in other areas.

9. Get going on a project. Nothing brings the team to life like an actual hands-on fixer.

10. Persist! Rome wasn't built in a day. J. Paul Getty didn't make his fortune overnight. Your dream team won't get off the ground at the first meeting. But keep at it and infuse others with your determination. You *will* get results!

CHAPTER 6

Making Low-Ball Offers That Sellers Will Accept

Handyman's special buyers always make the lowest offers. It only stands to reason. By the time you add up your acquisition and reselling costs, your fixing-up expenses and your hoped-for profit, you must offer low. Usually your offer will be significantly lower than that of other homebuyers who either may not have as sharp a pencil as you, or simply want to purchase a place in which to live and may not be thinking of doing much fix-up work. (Never underestimate the conditions in which people are willing to live.)

To get a good deal for yourself, you simply must "low-ball" the seller. (If you're still not sure why, reread Chapter 4.) Pay too much and you'll be making the seller very happy, but disappointing yourself.

Here's how to get your low-ball offer accepted.

A Winning Offer?

If you've ever tried to buy a fixer, you'll appreciate the following true story. Sidney and Leslie wanted to buy in the Piedmont area of Oakland, a very prestigious neighborhood which, unfortunately, even though the market was down, also had prestigious prices. The couple simply couldn't afford a home that was in good shape, so they looked for a cosmetic fixer, one with a lower price that needed simple work they could handle.

Eventually, after nearly four months of searching, they located an old two-story house that had fallen into disrepair. The plumbing and electrical systems seemed up to snuff, but the house appeared to need a new furnace, complete repainting inside and out and many new fixtures. It had been a rental and the tenants had taken the home to task over the years.

The out-of-town owner lived across the state and said (via his agent) that he was anxious to sell, but gave no specifics. So Sidney and Leslie made what they considered a reasonable offer. After checking out the property and doing their homework (described in Chapter 4), they offered $275,000, which was $75,000 less than the owner was asking.

The owner was outraged. He said that homes in the area regularly sold for $300,000 and higher. Sidney and Leslie's low offer was nothing more than an attempt to steal the property. But he then countered at $300,000—$50,000 less than he had been asking!

Sidney and Leslie were tempted. They wanted the house for more than just fixing up; they wanted it to live in it, hopefully for a long time. However, they simply couldn't afford to pay the $300,000 plus the costs of fixing up so it would be ready to move in. Their offer of $275,000 was what they could afford and they said so (through their agent).

The owner said he wanted a couple of weeks to think about it. If they'd leave the offer open-ended, he'd let them know.

They refused. They gave him 24 hours to decide yes or no. If it was no, they would then look elsewhere.

The owner countered again at $290,000, then yet again at $285,000. Eventually, he agreed to Sidney and Leslie's $275,000 offer, provided they could close the deal in 30 days, which they just managed to do.

Why Was the Deal Made?

It's nice to hear stories about how people successfully get a low-ball price for a good fixer property. However, if you're going to duplicate what was done here, it's important that you understand the story behind the story. Let's take a look at why the seller was willing to drop the price $75,000 for Sidney and Leslie.

1. Appearance—As noted in Chapter 2, cosmetic fixers can be some of the worst-appearing properties. Typically they need paint, have holes in the walls, broken windows, missing or destroyed appliances and ravaged yards. They just look bad. Hence, it's hard to get 95 percent of homebuyers to even consider them. The only people who will usually make offers are those, such as yourself, who are looking for a fixer.

2. Absentee Owner—Our buyers knew the owner lived half-way across the state. It would be difficult for him to get to where the house was and to supervise clean-up and fix-up work. To get it done, he'd have to hire a crew and trust them to do the work. Further, during the time they were working on the job, it would be difficult to sell. And finally, if he had a clap-trap job

done, it still wouldn't look good and wouldn't be that much easier to sell for a good price. In other words, the owner's fix-up options were limited.

3. Unrealistically High Asking Price—The owner realized the property was overpriced. He and his agent knew that similar properties were selling for "over $300,000." That was still considerably less than the $350,000 he was asking. The owner had already prepared himself to take much less. It's important to remember that very often a seller will know what a house is worth, yet will still ask considerably more, hoping to get a foolish buyer to pay their higher price.

4. Recession Market—At the time, the market was in a recession. That meant prices were level or declining slightly and that there were few buyers. It was a great time to be a purchaser, a terrible time to be a seller. If the owner wanted to get out, he would have to carefully consider *every* offer that came in, for there might not be another.

5. Persistent, Confident Buyers—Our buyers, Sidney and Leslie, hung tough. They didn't respond to the owner's attempts to get them to bump up the price. They didn't fall for the "open-ended offer" ploy, which would have essentially meant that the seller could hold onto their offer while hoping and waiting for another, better offer to come in.

But, perhaps the biggest factor of all in the sale, one that Sidney and Leslie did not know, was the motivation of the seller.

They later discovered that the seller had inherited the house from an uncle who had died a few years earlier. The seller had simply wanted to get his cash out. He didn't want to be an absentee landlord, he didn't want to fix up the

---

Rule

Find out WHY the seller wants out and you'll be half-way toward getting your low-ball offer accepted.

---

property and he didn't want to wait for a better market. He just wanted his cash and he wanted it now.

In the above example, we've seen how circumstances, property condition and the right buying stance can allow you to purchase a fixer at a price you believe is fair. These all worked for Sidney and Leslie, however, largely because of the seller's motivation. A less-motivated seller might have found other alternatives than dropping his price more than 20 percent.

How Do You Find Out the Seller's Motivation?

For Sidney and Leslie, the vital hidden factor in the transaction was the seller's motivation. If the seller had been living in or nearby the property; had the energy and time to fix it up, even minimally; or didn't want to get out quickly, the low-ball offer probably would not have been accepted. As it turned out, buyer stubbornness made up for not knowing the seller's motivation.

This, however, won't always be the way things work out for you. You could write up a dozen offers and get shot down a dozen times, even though your price was right for the property's condition, just because the seller was not highly motivated. If there's a single overriding factor that you need to know when attempting to get a low offer accepted on a fixer, it's why the seller has the property on the market. Find out that information and you will know whether you have a real chance, or whether you're just shooting in the dark.

How do you find out? One good way is to just ask. Even though the seller was out of town, Sidney and Leslie could easily have gotten his phone number. Or they could have even driven to see him.

They could have shown up to present their offer or one of their counter-offers. Or earlier on, they could have dropped in as potential buyers interested in his property. It's a rare seller who will turn away a serious buyer.

That's why I advise speaking directly to the seller. Always ask this point-blank question: "Why are you selling?"

Most times, it has been my experience for the seller to give an honest (or near-honest) answer. The seller in our example might have mentioned that he inherited the house and didn't want to bother with it. If *I* were the seller, I wouldn't have mentioned just how anxious I was to dump the place, but in a direct meeting, a seller may often admit this as well. The best and quickest way you have of finding out the seller's motivation is to simply ask.

You can also ask others. You can ask the agent (who may or may not be candid about this). You can ask tenants and neighbors, who may know (or who may *think* they know!).

Finally, you can judge by what the seller does. If the seller counters with a big cut in the selling price (as was the case here), you have a pretty good idea he's anxious. A seller who is not anxious will often counter at a price very close to what he was asking, hoping that your low-ball offer was just a trial balloon. A desperate seller, however, won't want to lose you and will try to get as low as possible to keep you hooked.

Have You Tried the Home Inspection Gambit?

There's another whole method of getting the seller to lower the price and that's to use a home inspection as a leveraging tool. Many people looking for fixers use this to their great advantage. Here's how this strategy works.

In today's market, it's almost a necessity to have a home inspection prior to the conclusion of the sale. Buyers want it so that they have a better idea of what they're purchasing. Sellers prefer it because it helps them after the sale to mitigate the buyer's complaints about problems with the property. If the buyer says, for example, "I never would have bought this property if I'd known it had a bad roof," the seller can respond, "You had it inspected. Blame your inspector, not me."

There are many ways to use the home inspection as leverage, but the most common is the following: The buyers, who are looking for a fixer, find a house and proceed to inspect it themselves. They determine just how much they can offer. And they approach the seller to find out his motivation.

They discover that the seller is not highly motivated. If the house doesn't sell this month, the seller figures it will sell next month or even next year. This is not the sort of seller who is usually willing to come down very much on price.

Now the buyers have to decide whether to (1) make their best low-ball offer for the property "as is," or (2) offer something higher and hope that the inspection will reveal damage that the seller may not be aware of. Then, they can renegotiate a lower price based on the inspection.

Offering the Low-Ball Price

Our buyers may offer their best low-ball price. They may write into the contract that they agree to buy "as is" and waive the right to an inspection. (You'd better be pretty darn sure of your guesstimates and those of your associates—see the last chapter—before going this route.)

If the house has a lot of damage, the seller may find this low-ball offer particularly appealing. Here are buyers who are making an offer and standing by it, regardless of the condition of the property. There aren't many buyers like this anymore. If I were a seller, I'd think three times before turning down or countering such an offer.

Going Higher Counting on the Inspection To Renegotiate

Or, the buyers could offer a higher price—one the seller is more likely to accept—and insist on an inspection. After the seller accepts, and when the inspection comes in revealing a lot of problems with the property, the buyers can then attempt to negotiate a lower price.

Note: If you use this second method, be sure that you *make the purchase contingent upon your inspection.* In other words, if you don't like what the inspection report says (regardless of what it says), you aren't committed to make the purchase.

Pros and Cons of Each Method

While the first method is more straightforward, it's less likely to snare a truly unmotivated seller. The seller may simply say that while your offer is appealing because you're accepting the house "as is," it's simply too low. This seller has the time to wait, hoping for a better offer to come by.

On the other hand, while the second method is disingenuous at worst, it's often more likely to get results because it forces the seller to consider the property's true problems. Potential buyers have made an offer to purchase, contingent on an inspection. But, once the inspection reveals its true terrible shape, they are only willing to buy at a reduced price. Even an unmotivated seller, in this second case, is likely to see that the price is going to have to be lowered, no matter when a buyer comes in, because of the property's condition.

Which Arguments Should You Use?

The problem with getting sellers to accept low-ball offers is that they just don't want to lose money. And even if the low-ball offer is still four times what they paid for the property years ago, if it's less than other similar homes are going for they just don't want to hear it. Many sellers would rather give away a good offer rather than accept it, if they thought it meant they were losing money on the deal. So, your task as a handyman's special buyer is to convince sellers that it's in their best interests to accept your offer. Here are the arguments you can use:

Arguments To Get a Lower Price

1. Condition   The first step in any negotiation over a fixer is to get consensus over the condition of the property. If you say it's run-down and a mess, but the seller says it looks fine to him, the deal is hopeless. You won't get anywhere in negotiations over price until the seller agrees with you about the true condition of the property. How do you get an intransigent seller to be realistic? Consider using the home inspection gambit just discussed.

2. Price Is Related to Condition   You must get the seller to accept the fact that no sane person is going to buy that property at full, great-shape price in its present condition. If the seller persists in believing that someone is going to ignore the home's problems and offer 25 to 30 percent more than the property is currently worth, you can be sympathetic. But, I would get out of there and get on to the next property. You can't reason with a fool.

3. It Costs a Lot To Fix Up   Once the seller agrees with you that the house is in terrible condition and acknowledges that a discount is in order, the only remaining question is how big a discount. I suggest bringing out the figures you've developed and explaining them in detail. If an associate is donating some work, point that out. Also, point out all the work you're doing and not directly charging for. In short, show the seller how much it will cost you to fix up the property. Get the seller to acknowledge that your figures are reasonable. (They had better be, else you could lose money on the job!)

4. Compare Your Fixing Up the Property to the Seller's Fixing It Up   Remember, if the seller fixes up the property, he will have to spend the time involved, perhaps months or even as much as a year, fixing up the place. During that time, the seller may not be able to live in the house, and almost certainly will not be able to rent it out. Further, current mortgage payments, taxes, insurance and other costs will continue to run. Finally, ask if the seller can afford to pay the costs? Usually fixing up means the person doing the work has to get financing to cover it. A new mortgage is not unusual. Can the seller get this financing? Does the seller want to?

Further, point out how much it's realistically going to cost the seller in time and money to fix up the property. And then what will the seller gain? After it's all fixed up, the seller must still find a buyer. And once that buyer is found, the price paid probably won't be far off from what you are offering PLUS the costs of fixing it up!

In short, the seller can save time, money and effort simply by selling to you now . . . and still get essentially the same amount as if they held on, fixed up and sold later!

5. There's the Hassle I always ask sellers point blank if they have ever done any fix-up work? Have they waited a half day, a day, a week or more for a worker or a subcontractor to show up, only to have the person come in, do a few hours of labor and then leave with that job still unfinished? It happens all the time.

What about work going on while they're trying to live in the property? There's always dust. The rain and dirt manage to come in. There's the noise. And don't think that because the tradespeople promise they'll only be at the job from 9 to 5, they'll stick to those hours. Expect them to show up at 7:00 a.m. and not leave until 9 at night. Yes, of course, they'll say they'll do it when you want it. But then they may not show up at all!

Most sellers have had at least a little bit of experience with having work done for them and, once reminded, they should quickly remember just how unpleasant it was. Keep reminding them of the hassle every time they get back to the high price they want.

These then are the arguments you can use to get sellers to lower their price to something more realistic for you. Will these arguments work every time? Certainly not. But, if you're convincing, they should work often enough to get you the property you want at the price you want.

Arguments To Get a Lower Price for a Handyman's Special

1. The property needs fixing up.

2. The price is directly related to the condition.

---

*R*ules for Getting Your Price

- Be reasonable.
- Treat the whole matter as business.
- Never take it personally.
- Don't ask for favors—you want the sellers to do what's best for them. That will be just right for you.

---

3. Fix-up costs are high.

4. Someone has to fix it up and the costs for everybody are going to be roughly the same.

5. The sellers can avoid the hassle of fixing it up by selling at a realistic price NOW!

CHAPTER 7

Structuring the Deal

It may seem that getting your property at the right price is the trickiest part of doing a handyman's special. After price, everything seems downhill. The truth is, however, that price is only the first step. There are many other pitfalls that can hurt you along the way to a successful deal. Certainly the next item to watch out for is structuring the deal.

What exactly do I mean by "structuring the deal"? Let me illustrate with a story that I still vividly remember of an auction that I participated in years ago. It was an estate sale of a home that had partially burnt down. The owner had died in the fire and now the property was being sold to the highest bidder.

In an estate sale, the executor or administrator will typically solicit bids for property to be sold and accept the highest. However, a court usually has to put its stamp of approval on the sale. This is done at an open hearing where the judge will typically open the bidding to anyone else, providing the next bid is a step (usually 10 percent) higher than the "accepted" bid. That's where the auction comes in.

Mine was the accepted bid. However, I was fairly certain that others would bid in open court because the property was such an attractive fixer. It was a fairly new house in a great neighborhood, with extensive cosmetic burn damage from the fire. (Very little of the basic structure itself was damaged, just the interior walls, ceilings, fixtures and so on.)

I was right. There were at least a half dozen other bidders and very quickly the bidding moved higher than I wanted to go. So following my rule that it is vitally important not to bid higher than my pencil calculates I can profit, I dropped out.

The winner was a young man who was ecstatic with his purchase. I felt he had bid too much, but that was his problem. What next ensued, however, bordered on the comic.

The successful bidder was required to immediately put up a cashier's check for 10 percent of the purchase price, with the balance to follow within two days. This fellow, however, wanted to use a personal check, which the court was not willing to accept. Further, he said he wanted to negotiate the balance so that he could pay interest only over the next six months while he fixed up the property. Then, when he resold it, he would pay off the balance.

The judge looked at the executor for about half a second before declaring the sale invalid and asking for the bidding to restart. All the bidders had remained, so we did it again, this time with a young woman winning, again bidding too high in my opinion.

She, however, was prepared. She had the cashier's check, had already arranged financing (which we'll discuss in Chapter 8) and agreed to pay the balance of the purchase price the next day. She also told us she had arranged for the work to be done and was quite sure it could be finished in no longer than five weeks. And she smugly indicated that she already had in mind a buyer for the resale!

I had to give her credit for her planning—she had totally structured the deal from beginning to end. She knew what she was doing and how to do it. But when I met her several years later, she confessed that she had, indeed, paid too much for the property. However, because she had a solid plan, she still ended up making at least a tiny amount of money. If she hadn't structured the deal properly, however, she would have lost a bundle.

Rule

If you have a good plan, you usually won't go astray when working with a handyman's special.

I call a good plan "structuring," and here are four elements to successfully structure the purchase of any fixer:

1. Time—Planning day-by-day how you will use it

2. Cash—Knowing where you'll get it from and exactly when you'll need it

3. Safety—Planning escape paths in case something goes wrong with the deal

4. Resale—Knowing, before you buy, how and when you'll sell

Notice that we're not limiting the "deal" strictly to the purchase agreement. Rather, the deal is the entire fixing up process, from purchase to ultimate resale.

Whenever you purchase a fixer, starting with your very first one, you want to structure your deal. You want to plan ahead so that every step, hopefully every possibility—good or bad—is covered. That's what we'll concentrate on helping you do in this chapter.

1. How You Control Time: The Logistics of Fixing Up

The first element in structuring your fix-up deal is working with time. Time often represents the biggest stumbling block for most people who get into the field.

Think of it in military terms. In order to fight a war, a general must have his army in the right place at the right time, along with all the right supplies for the army to do its job. Further, "the right place" changes every day. Making all this happen is called logistics, which is the science and art of procuring, maintaining and transporting military equipment and personnel.

Fixing up a property is, in some respects, just like a military campaign. It starts when you buy the property and involves getting cash and financing in the right amounts and at the right times to secure the purchase and to pay for the repair work. It also involves getting work done in the right order so that one project doesn't bump into another and so that you don't end up having to do things over and over. (For example, you don't want to paint before you finish plastering the walls.)

A fixer is essentially a logistics job. You need to know what needs to be done, where and, most important, WHEN. But since a fixer often takes months, sometimes half a year or longer, how do you organize all this? How do you keep track of the myriad different chores that need to be done without losing one or two in the shuffle? The handyman's specials field is rife with stories of people who didn't do the right things at the right time and paid dearly for it.

For example, I can remember a friend who was doing a fix-up job in the autumn and got so involved in inside work that he forgot to get the roof repaired. He was caught by winter's first rain and had a lot of water damage. Another friend of mine concentrated on getting the inside of the property perfect and ready for resale, only to realize she had forgotten to plant a lawn and landscape the outside, something that can take several months (if you do it inexpensively by seed). To get a timely sale, she had to transplant grown bushes and trees and have sod carted in—an incredibly expensive undertaking.

Create a Working Time Line

My personal solution to a fixer's logistics challenge is to create a working time line. I plot, in advance and day by day, everything that I anticipate I'll need to do. Further, as new needs develop, I put them on my time line.

I use a 12-month calendar, many varieties of which are available from any good stationary store. My calendar shows 12 months at a glance and leaves enough room for writing information in on every date.

On this time line, I can graphically indicate everything that needs to be done, as far as I know at the moment. My suggestion is that you consider doing something similar. You may want a wall-hanging calendar like I use, or you may use one of the many computer programs that are available to create something similar. (I like the paper variety because I can easily see it all at once. The computer version, however, allows you unlimited space for writing notes on any given day.)

As we go through this book, particularly when it comes to the actual work you'll need to do, you'll want to note your time line very heavily. When will you work on the kitchen? The bath? When will you call in the roofers? And so on. But for this chapter, we're going to consider the time line only in general terms of the overall structure of the deal.

How To Plan the Overall Deal on the Time Line

I suggest that you plot on your time line such things as the following. (Note: These are minimums. You will certainly add many more as you develop the time line for each fixer you do.)

---

*I*tems for Your Time Line

1. The day you'll raise the seed money (cash) you'll need for the deal

2. The day you'll prearrange for the financing (the mortgage)

3. The day you'll make the offer (Note: The first three items take place BEFORE you buy the property.)

4. The day the offer is accepted

5. The day you need to have your mortgage funded

6. The day you need to deposit the final money into escrow (and the amount)

7. The day you'll take possession

8. The day fix-up work will start

9. The days that you'll need money for different fix-up projects

10. The days your mortgage payments are due

---

11. The days property taxes and insurance payments are due

12. The day you anticipate work will be completed (covered in Part 3 of this book)

13. When you'll put the house up for sale

14. How long before you anticipate you'll be able to sell

With a realistic and complete time line, you will avoid the biggest fixer pitfall of all—surprises. Of course, you can't anticipate everything. But you will have planned out the big things, particularly when you'll need money for various parts of your project.

2. Cash

We're going to assume here that you're able to get financing (a mortgage) to handle both the purchase and the work on your fix-up property. (We'll cover how this is done in Chapter 8.) What we're concerned about here is *when* you'll need the money and in what proportions of cash to financing. Let's look at it from the cash perspective, first.

Coming Up with Cash

Cash means real money out of your own pocket or someone else's. It is the hardest money to come by. Naturally, you want to use as little of your own as possible. Many people believe they won't need any of their own money. (Indeed, a number of authors have made a good living by telling people how they can purportedly make a fortune in real estate by buying properties with no money down.)

The truth of the matter is that you will need some cash of your own. Depending on how you structure the deal, however, you may not need a great amount. The key is to get as many other people to put up as much cash as possible.

What Will You Need Cash For?

You'll need to come up with cash for a variety of things at many different times. Here's a partial list:

1. Cash for planning the deal

2. Cash for a down payment on purchase

3. Cash for closing costs on purchase

4. Cash to buy materials and hire labor during fix-up

5. Cash for incidentals, such as building permits, at the start of fix-up

6. Cash for mortgage payments while you work on the project

7. Cash for year-end taxes and insurance

8. Cash to live on while you work on the project

When you add up all of these amounts, you will quickly see that you need an enormous amount of cash at many different times to do the whole fixer deal. It can add up to tens of thousands of dollars, sometimes hundreds of thousands. Will you have that money available? And just as important, will it be ready when you'll need it?

If you're like most of us, you don't have much cash on hand. Therefore, you'll need to arrange for cash from other sources at different times. For example, you'll need a big infusion of cash when you make the purchase to cover the down payment, closing costs and fees incidental to starting the fix-up work. Then you'll need additional ongoing infusions of cash to handle the work and perhaps even to handle your living expenses.

Cash Before the Deal

I call this "seed money" and it's number one in the above list. This is money that you'll need to cover your own expenses while you look for property. When you call someone in and pay for them to do an inspection and then you don't buy the property, you'll need seed money to pay them for their efforts. (If you do buy the property, they are usually paid when the purchase goes through.) If you call a meeting of your dream team and order coffee and donuts, you'll need to pay for those, too.

Seed money is very important and it's money you need to come up with *by yourself.* It would be an embarrassment as well as a serious weakening of your position in the eyes of others if you tried to get someone else to pay for this. Sometimes the amount you'll need may be fairly small, only a few hundred dollars. But, you'll need to spend it at a time when you probably won't see any immediate promise of results.

int

"**S**eed money" in reality is faith money.
You put it up on faith.
You use it to bet on yourself.

A word of advice: In a sense, this seed money is the most important cash you can spend, because it establishes you in the eyes of others as well as helps you to more clearly appraise a property. Some people, however, scrimp here because they can't see the light at the end of the tunnel. They take a potential ally or associate out to breakfast, but don't want to buy them the best meal. Now, how does that look to the other person? If you can't afford or don't want to spend even such a small amount of money, what does that say about your confidence in yourself? Or about your confidence in your ability to put together a good fixer deal?

So don't scrimp on the little stuff. If necessary, be flamboyant. It will come back to you a thousand times over, even if you can't see results at the moment.

Cash at Time of Purchase

You can only legally come up with cash from two sources: savings and borrowings. Therefore, to reduce the amount of cash you need to take from your savings, you must increase your borrowing. Your first need for this will come with the down payment and closing costs.

While you most likely will get an institutional mortgage (from a savings and loan, bank, mortgage banker, or other institution) for the majority of the purchase price, these lenders won't normally loan 100 percent of the purchase price. Rather, they'll only loan a percentage, typically 80 percent. (We'll have more to say about this in Chapter 8.)

So, for your down payment, you'll probably need to come up with about 20 percent cash. If the property you are buying costs $100,000, that's $20,000 in cash, plus perhaps another $5,000 including closing costs, for a total of $25,000, and we're just at the beginning. How can you structure the deal to reduce the amount of initial cash you'll require?

How Do You Put in Less of Your Own Money?

You can put in less cash by doing any of the following:

1. Get a higher institutional mortgage, better than 80 percent. It's difficult, but not impossible.

2. Get the seller to carry either the whole mortgage or a second mortgage. If the seller carries a second mortgage for 10 or 15 percent of the purchase price, your cash requirement for the down payment drops to only 10 or 5 percent ($10,000 or as little as $5,000 in our example).

3. Get the seller to pay for your closing costs. There's no rule that a seller can't pay your closing costs. If the seller agrees to this, you save more of your cash. (In our example, you would save an additional $5,000.) The seller may agree to increase the price slightly and finance your closing costs. (See Chapter 8 for details on how this might be done.)

4. Arrange for the cash you need from relatives or friends. You may be able to get others to put up part or even all of the money at the time of purchase in exchange for a promise to repay or even a percentage of the profits later on. Be aware, however, that institutional lenders will not give a mortgage if the down payment is borrowed. (Again, see Chapter 8 for solutions to this problem.)

5. Form a partnership. In the previous chapter, we talked about putting together a dream team. You may be able to rely on your team for part or all of the initial money that you need.

How To Arrange for Cash During Fix-Up

In addition to the cash you'll need at the time you actually purchase the property, you'll also need cash during the weeks and months you are fixing it up. Hopefully, you'll be able to accurately predict just when this money is needed. Now the question is, where do you get it?

You can get cash during the fix-up from any of these sources:

1. Your Savings—Many people who do fixers prefer to pay for all of the labor, materials, mortgage payments and other costs out of their own funds. They reason that this way they aren't beholden to anyone, they don't have to agree to anyone else's terms, they don't have to pay interest on the money if it's borrowed and they don't have to worry about the money being available just when needed. I prefer to do fix-up work this way myself, when possible. After all, I know that I'll get it all back, and more, upon sale.

2. Borrow the Money You'll Need—You may be able to borrow what you need from the seller. Or, you may arrange for a construction or home equity loan from an institutional lender. Check out Chapter 8 for details.

3. Get Some of It in Trade—If you have a dream team, you may arrange to have much of the labor and even materials traded out for a share of the profits. But be careful if you do this. It seems like everyone always wants a bigger share of profits than their work warrants.

4. Take in Partners—As we've seen, your dream team members may be willing to contribute, as may friends and family. Again, however, this means you'll end up with a smaller share of the pie on sale.

Should You Make Your Cash Arrangements in Advance?

No matter how you arrange for the cash you'll need to do the deal, what's vitally important is that you arrange for it at the right time. It won't do you any good to get money for a mortgage payment or to pay a roofer three months after you need it. You need money on time.

What's important to remember is that you aren't the only one who knows this. Lenders, whether institutional or private, instinctively know it as well. This means that if you go looking for money after the time you need it, they'll find out. (It's hard to keep desperation out of your eyes or the way you speak.) And if they discover that you didn't plan ahead, they'll take that to mean that you don't really know what you're doing, that your other plans (including repayment) may be flawed and that you may be a lost cause. Would *you* lend money to a person like that?

Let's take an example to see what *not* to do.

Janine bought a small three-bedroom, one-bath home in a nice area of town. It was technically a "broken-back" fixer. Cosmetically it looked okay, but it had only one bathroom. The same home with two baths sold in the same area for around $35,000 more. Janine figured she would put in another bath for around $10,000 and then resell for a profit.

The problem was that she used up so much of her own funds making the purchase that half-way through the fix-up, she ran out of cash. She immediately went out and tried to borrow.

But by then, the house was hacked apart and no lender wanted to make a loan when there was evidence of prior construction (else their mortgage could be in jeopardy because of a mechanic's lien). Banks also didn't want to make any personal loans because they were suspicious of her ability to repay now that she didn't have any more cash of her own and was fully committed, financially speaking, to the existing mortgage. Her friends and family felt the same way, although they were more sympathetic. They said they just didn't have any money they could lend her.

Within a few weeks, Janine was in serous danger of losing her property because she couldn't make the mortgage payment. She considered giving up work on the house (which she was doing full-time) and getting a regular job, at least a part-time job. The trouble with that solution was it would take several weeks for her to get cash flowing and during this time her fix-up work would slow or stop, payments would mount, and she'd be even further behind.

Janine's problem was not so much lack of cash as it was planning. If she had structured the deal so that from the onset she had overestimated rather than underestimated the required cash flow, things would have worked out. If she had arranged for an additional loan at the beginning, she wouldn't have had trouble at the end.

Rule

Always remember that banks, friends and associates are usually willing to lend you money when you don't really need it. It's when you're desperate that they won't let you have it!

This story does, however, have a happy ending. In our society, plastic almost always comes to the rescue. Janine had two credit cards and was able to quickly arrange for two more. By taking cash withdrawals, she was able to cover her expenses and save the deal. However, she had to pay very hefty interest charges (more than 20 percent), which ate into her profits.

I share this story to suggest that you'll do far better when fixing up if you use your time line to plan when you'll need money and then arrange for it *far in advance* of the need.

Thus far we've been concerned with timing and cash. However, there are other elements to structuring a deal that can be important, particularly if they are left out or if you don't deal with them correctly. I call them safety valves and you need to pay particular attention to each.

3. Safety: Structuring in a Contingency Safety Valve

This refers to the sales agreement itself as opposed to the overall deal (which includes not only the purchase, but also all the fixing up and the later reselling). In the sales agreement, you have the opportunity to put in contingent clauses. These are statements that say something such as, "This purchase is subject to the buyer obtaining financing . . . " and then giving the terms of the financing you're looking for.

As a buyer of handyman's specials, I always want to leave as many escape hatches for myself as possible. I always include contingency clauses that allow me to back out of the deal gracefully (without having the seller sue me or keep my deposit).

Why do I want these? There are many reasons, but the two best are that with a fixer it seems that you are continually finding new work that needs to be done as the purchase progresses and arranging financing tends to be tricky. Let's consider some new problems that tend to crop up.

Remember that a typical purchase usually takes a month or longer to complete. During that time, you may inspect the property several times and each time you do, something new may pop up. What do you do, for example, if the deal is ready to close and you discover a big crack in the heat transfer box of the furnace or a leak in the roof? With a standard transaction, the buyer typically gets only one shot at an inspection and if nothing shows then, it's too bad. With a fixer, however, I always make sure I have the right to go back many times, to measure, to check things out in greater detail and so on.

I also include a contingency clause written into the sales agreement that states the purchase is subject to there being no additional undiscovered or undisclosed problems before the close of escrow (when the title transfers to you). If there are, then the deal is open to renegotiation, or I don't have to buy.

Financing Contingencies

The same holds true with financing. In a regular purchase, the financing is usually straightforward. The buyer is obtaining a mortgage for a set amount of money. However, in a handyman's special deal, often the buyer is not only obtaining a mortgage for the purchase, but may also be obtaining a construction loan (either separately or blended with the purchase mortgage) to do the fix-up work. While the purchase mortgage may come through (not the funding, but the initial acceptance of buyer) fairly quickly, it may not be until the last day before the construction loan is approved. And I don't want the property unless I can get a construction loan.

Therefore, a contingency clause that makes the purchase subject to my obtaining financing for both purchase *and* fix-up construction protects my hide.

Other Contingency Clauses

You may want other contingency clauses structured into the sales agreement depending on the type of property you're buying. For example, your purchase may be contingent on an adjoining piece of property being zoned commercial or being rezoned residential. Your agreement could be contingent on how tenants leave the property after they move out. In short, there's no limit to the number of different kinds of contingencies you may want.

---

*C*aution

Every time you structure a contingency clause into the sales agreement, it protects you and gives you a better deal BUT it weakens and gives the seller a worse deal. Hence, add too many clauses and the seller won't accept. Indeed, sometimes contingency clauses are actually a trade-off with price. In order to get your price, you may be forced to accept virtually none of them!

Also, unless you're experienced and knowledgeable in real estate, don't attempt to write the contingency clauses yourself. Have a competent attorney or real estate agent do it. You might have the best of intentions, but you could find you've created an unfulfillable condition or forgot to include a method for removing a clause.

Do You Have a Rental Option?

Another safety valve that I try to structure into fixer deals has nothing to do with the sales agreement. Rather, it has everything to do with how the fix-up work is planned.

What if, despite the best of planning, your funds for fixing up don't arrive as anticipated? Or what if you get sick during the fixing-up stage and can't complete the work you had intended to do yourself? Or what if the market for the property suddenly deteriorates (as has happened in many areas over the past decade) and it becomes clear you won't be able to resell for what you had anticipated?

One option I like to keep open is the possibility of renting out the property. Any property that is habitable can be rented. The word "habitable" is the key. If you've knocked out the kitchen or the toilets or if it has an uncovered roof, it's just not habitable. The rest of the time, however, it is. Often, if work in areas that affect habitability has to cease, the place can be made rentable with only a few days modifying work.

I always try to structure the fix-up so that the property is uninhabitable for the barest minimum amount of time. Of course, I could be planning to live in it myself. However, even if not, I want to be able to switch horses in midstream, so to speak. I want to be able to stop fixing the property up and working toward a sale and instead get it in shape to rent.

A few years ago, I bought a home that was in terrible shape. Not only was it cosmetically a mess needing repainting, recarpeting and so on, it also needed to be completely replumbed and have new wiring put in.

I anticipated it would be vacant for three to five months while all this work was done. However, no sooner had I completed the purchase than a janitor at a nearby church approached me with a proposal. He said he and his family would be willing to move in, at three-fourths normal rent. He wanted the place for a year.

During his time in the house, he would do many of the handyman chores that were required. His vocation was a janitor, and so he offered to do the painting and all of the cleaning. He'd agree to be gone for the few days when the water had to be absolutely shut off. The rest of the time the plumbing work could be done in stages with only part of house incapacitated. He'd do the same for the electrical work.

In short, I could collect rent from the moment I bought the house, plus get some of the labor thrown into the bargain. The house wouldn't be vacant until it was ready to sell.

How long do you think I considered his offer?

He moved in the first week and during the course of the year, the house was fixed up and all of its problems cured. Eventually he did move out and I did sell. Looking back, I realize that we helped each other. He got a place to live at a reduced rent. I got rental income and quality labor.

Rule

Never overlook the rental option.
Sometimes it can save you money.
Sometimes it can save the deal.

Is the Land Value There?

Yet another safety valve, particularly when you're dealing with a severely distressed fixer, is to pay particular attention to the land's intrinsic value. This is especially the case where there are structural problems. Here's an example where not paying close attention trapped the buyer in the deal.

My friend Shelley recently bought a home in a very nice section of Los Angeles. While most of Los Angeles is fairly flat, some homes, particularly in the more desirable areas, are built on the sides of hills. Unfortunately, the area is subject to flooding and earthquakes, which means that those hills have a tendency to occasionally move down into the flatland.

The home Shelley bought had been damaged by the 1993 Northridge earthquake, although the property was not in that area. The earth had slid down during the quake and a mound had suddenly been upthrust through the center of the house, effectively dividing it in half. While each half was basically intact, the house as a whole had been condemned and written off by both the insurance company and the owner as a total loss. Needless to say, Shelley was able to buy it for a song with the seller financing the sale and Shelley only putting 10 percent down.

After she spent ample time patting herself on the back for her low-priced purchase, she then set about fixing up the house. After many hours arguing with the building department, she got them to agree to a set of plans that called for several concrete trusses to be built under the remains of the existing two halves. Then, using her own money, she had the trusses built and placed and carefully had the two halves levered back into place and nailed together. It was an altogether creative solution to an apparently unsolvable problem. After some cosmetic work, the house looked great. You'd never know it had been a disaster. Then she put it up for sale.

Her problems began when her potential buyers tried to get financing. Lenders all seemed aware of the problems that had occurred with the house and knew that it was still on insubstantial soil. The regular institutional lenders (like banks and savings and loans) wouldn't make a loan. When the only financing the buyers could get was from high-risk lenders who wanted a higher-than-market interest rate plus extra points, they were alerted to the seriousness of the problem and were scared off.

Shelley was eventually able to find other buyers who were willing to accept the house's problems and the higher-than-usual financing, for a significant reduction in price. However, now Shelley found that it was impossible to obtain even minimal homeowner's fire and earthquake insurance on the property, and even the high-risk lender wouldn't lend without those. And so the second sale fell through.

Eventually, Shelley was forced to rent out the property. The problem was she had used her own funds—a substantial amount—for the down payment and for the fix-up and was now unable to get the money out. She was stuck.

The moral here is that Shelley didn't look at the underlying value of the land. She only looked at the improvements, the house and the problem. Yes, she found a solution for those. But the underlying value (or lack of value) of the land hadn't changed. It basically was a valueless or extremely low-value property. She had been trapped.

Whenever you are considering buying a fixer, one of the safety valves you should check is the land itself. The way to check is to ask yourself, "If things go terribly wrong, can I always sell the land, hopefully for most of what I have put into the property?" If the answer is no, look elsewhere.

You need the safety valve of land that is saleable. Be particularly careful when you buy property that is

- on hillsides,

- in flood plains,

- adjoining factories or large commercial developments,

- near dump sites and

- near or on property formerly used for gas stations or a landfill.

You want to be able to *resell the land alone,* if worse comes to worst. You don't want to be told that a lender or insurer or government agency will block the sale.

4. Resale

Smart real estate people always say that you make your money when you buy, not when you sell. What they mean by this is that you can't get more than market price when you resell (unless, of course, you are extremely lucky). Thus, you need to know that market price in advance and then purchase accordingly. (We've already seen this in terms of property appraisal in Chapter 4.)

However, proper deal structuring goes even farther than just having a sense of what the property should sell for a year or more down the road. It offers a plan for the resale.

Your resale plan can take several avenues. We'll consider these three: Finding a buyer early, working with an agent and selling by owner.

How Can You Find a Buyer Early?

You'll recall from our example of the auction (earlier in this chapter) that the successful bidder had a potential buyer in mind even before she bid on the property. That's the ultimate way to handle resale. But how can you do this?

I have some friends who not only fix up properties on the side, but also manage rentals for others (they have real estate licenses, which are usually required to run a property management firm). They manage over a hundred rental houses, condos and apartments. In the process, they talk with a great number of renters, many of whom would just love to own property.

One of the things they do is keep a list of tenants who would like to be owners and who have the savings, income and good credit to make a purchase. When they structure a deal to buy a fixer, they often have one or more of these tenants in mind.

My friends will often speak to selected tenants before and during the fix-up work. They'll bring the tenants (who may be living in anything from an apartment to a house) out to the fixer property and show them the quality of the workmanship. They try to build enthusiasm in these tenants and it often succeeds. Thus, by the time they are ready to sell the fixer, their buyer is ready to go.

You, of course, are probably not going to be managing rental property. But, if you put together a dream team as outlined in Chapter 5, undoubtedly at least one of your team members is likely to have some connection with rentals. Speak to that person early on and see who they can convert from a tenant to a buyer. If you do your homework, you could have your fixer presold!

Should You Be Working with an Agent?

In addition to trying to get a tenant converted to a buyer, you should structure your deal so that you're simultaneously working with one or more agents. (You really can't count on a tenant making the move, so you need other options.)

If you have an agent as part of your dream team, that person should be involved early on, talking up the property to other agents and looking for buyers. If you don't have an agent on your dream team (or don't have a team), then you may want to find a good agent to work with you on the resale.

Bring this agent in early on. You may want to list the property several months before it's actually finished, telling the agent that you'll be willing to sell for a little less to any buyer who commits early. Or you may want to wait until the work is totally finished before letting potential buyers see the project. Savvy investors who do fixers on a regular basis know they'll get top dollar if they wait until they can show off the finished home.

In either case, however, you want your agent on board early and talking up the property to other agents in the area. You want to use your agent's networking abilities, as these are probably the key to finding you a buyer.

Should You Sell by Yourself?

Finally, you may want to structure your deal so that, at the end, you sell FSBO (For Sale By Owner), without the services of an agent. If you go this route, you're going to want to prepare early on. While you're fixing up, you may want at minimum to have a sign in the front yard announcing that the property is for resale. You never know who in the neighborhood may be interested and might stop by to inquire.

You will also want to allocate some time, particularly near the end of the work phase, when you will attempt to develop buyers. You will need time to put together a flier describing the property and post it on bulletin boards in the area. You may want to put together a short video on your property and see if the local access television channel will accept it. (Local access TV often takes almost anything that people put together with a simple camcorder.)

Finally, when selling the property yourself, you will need to allocate money *after* the work is completed for newspaper advertising and for mortgage, tax and insurance payments while the property remains empty until it's sold.

Note: Some handyman's special investors think they can rent out the property after fix-up is complete, and find a buyer at the same time. Don't count on it. It's very difficult to get a tenant to do a good job showing a property. Most are unwilling to do so because it impinges on their quiet enjoyment of the premises. Yes, consider renting as a safety valve. But no, don't rent as part of your resale plan. Instead, have enough time and dollars socked away to handle expenses associated with the property during the resale period.

CHAPTER 8

How To Get Financing

The name of the game in real estate—and particularly with regard to fixers—is financing. I know of no one in the field (and I've been in it for over 30 years) who works on a strictly cash basis. Everyone borrows to make their deals and I'm sure you're no exception.

Handyman's specials, however, present special problems when it comes to finding money. Some lenders won't touch them. Other lenders will only give reduced mortgage amounts at higher interest rates and with more points. And many borrowers don't always have sterling credit. In this chapter, we're going to deal with these and related problems and see how to overcome them.

Is 100 Percent Financing Possible?

This is probably the number-one question with regard to borrowing. The answer is yes, it is possible. But, there are so many strings attached that you may not want it.

Real estate financing in general (as with most financing) is set up on the basis of risk and reward. Naturally, the lenders want to minimize their risk and at the same time maximize their reward. Over the years they have discovered that the best way to do this is to only make real estate loans to individuals who are committed to the property on which the mortgage is offered.

And how do you show commitment to a property? By putting *your own money* into the pot. Lenders feel that if the borrowers have some of their own money involved, they are much more likely to fight to save that property by making the mortgage payments (the lender's reward) and avoiding foreclosure (the lender's risk).

---

*H*int

Lenders are in the business of loaning money, not owning property. The very last thing they want is to take a property back through foreclosure. That's why they try to be as careful as possible when making the loan, to be sure the borrower can and will repay.

How much money do lenders feel that the borrower should put into the property? Technically, the amount should be enough to cover any lender's loss in the event of foreclosure and that usually works out to about 20 percent of the purchase price, assuming property values don't drop. In the back of a lender's mind, however, is the thought that with one-fifth of the price put up by the borrower, there's a very low chance that person will default. They simply have too much to lose.

Therefore, be aware that in asking for 100 percent financing, you are breaking a cardinal rule that most lenders strictly believe because you're not putting any of your own money into the deal. As far as they are concerned, lending money to you is tantamount to throwing kerosene on a fire!

Can You Get 100 Percent Financing from a Seller?

Having just said that lenders don't, in principle, like the idea of making 100 percent loans, let's now go on to see how 100 percent financing might still be possible. Let's start with the seller.

The seller is always your best source of financing. The trouble is that the vast majority of sellers want to get their cash out or are in no position to finance your purchase. But not all sellers. Occasionally you'll find a seller who owns a property free and clear or who owes just a small amount. With the right amount of convincing, you might just be able to get this seller to finance your purchase of his property. Here's how Lou did it.

Lou found a small cottage by the beach that had been on the market a long time. Stan, an old retired fellow, owned the place and wanted to sell it and move to the desert where the warm climate would help his asthma. It turned out that Stan had a hefty retirement and really didn't need any cash from the sale. He just wanted out of the property. (He didn't want the bother of renting it out and felt an obligation to stay in it until it was sold.)

The land near the beach was extremely valuable, although the cottage itself was old, dilapidated and in Lou's opinion, worthless. The deal was a "scraper."

Lou quickly learned that financing the purchase from institutional lenders such as banks or savings and loans would be hopeless. Most wouldn't lend at all because the value was in the lot, not the building. Those that would lend were only willing to give a maximum of 70 percent. Further, most said they wouldn't "subordinate" (make their loan secondary) to the new construction loan Lou needed to put up a new house.

So Lou offered this proposal to Stan, the seller. Stan would give Lou 100 percent financing on the purchase of the property. In essence, he would turn it over to Lou. Further, Stan would agree to subordinate his mortgage to a new construction loan.

Lou would then get a construction loan, scrape the existing cottage off the property, put up a beautiful, large new home and sell it. At the time of the sale, Lou would pay off Stan, the seller.

Stan considered the proposal. But, because he wasn't born yesterday, he asked some questions. He asked, "What if we do this deal and then something happens to you and you don't put up the new house? You could get sick! Or some other, better financial deal could come up! Where would I be then? I could foreclose, but my house would be gone!"

Lou thought about it and told Stan that it probably would be easier to sell an empty lot than the lot with the old cottage on it, and probably for the same money! Stan would be taking a risk, but Lou pledged that he would do the work if it were humanly possible. He then showed Lou his track record of seven previous, similar jobs.

Stan nodded, then asked, "But, what if you do put up the house and it's lovely, but the market is bad? Or the house turns out to cost too much for the area? What if you just can't sell it? I could foreclose, but then I'd end up with a big house and a big construction loan on which I couldn't make the payments. Wouldn't I be in real trouble then?"

Lou had to agree that Stan was asking some shrewd questions. He also had to acknowledge that Stan would be at risk by doing this deal. He'd be at risk when the lot was cleared, during construction and until the new home sold. Lou then asked if Stan was willing to do the deal if he received a percentage of the profits. In other words, would the risk be worthwhile to Stan if the rewards were high enough?

Stan considered. He said that at the very worst, even if he lost the property completely, he would still have his retirement and he'd be okay. On the other hand, if he could make a bigger profit on the deal, he'd like that. "What do you have in mind?" he asked Lou.

Lou then suggested the following. He would do the deal, scrape the cottage, put up the house and then sell it. In addition to the sales price, Lou would show Stan all his costs and then his profit. He would then give Stan 20 percent of his profits.

Stan chuckled and said he wasn't born yesterday. "No disrespect, young man, but there's no way I could know whether the numbers you were showing me were true or false." Then Stan made a proposal. He suggested that Lou pay him 20 percent more for the property up front and do the same deal. The risks were still the same to Stan, yet he'd know up front what his extra reward was.

Lou thought that over, but decided that a 20 percent increase in the purchase price of the property was much more than 20 percent of the profits later on. They dickered and finally compromised at 13 percent.

Stan and Lou did the deal, the house was scraped, a new one was put up and it was sold and the money split as agreed.

Stan went off to a drier climate and Lou, as far as I know, is still doing fixer-upper deals.

Rule

Yes, you can get 100 percent financing from a seller. But, unless the seller is a total fool, you'll have to give up some of your profits to get it.

You may end up giving up a percentage at the back end or paying more at the front end. In our example, Stan generously (some might say foolishly because of the risk) agreed to the entire financing. In most cases, the seller will insist on your putting some cash into the deal.

Nevertheless, seller financing—sometimes 100 percent seller financing—is not only possible, but *the best possible* way to handle many deals.

Can You Get 100 Percent Financing from Lenders other than the Seller?

Again the answer is yes, but it's far trickier.

First off, keep in mind that institutional lenders are far stricter with loans to investors than they are to those who intend to live in the property. For example, if you tell a lender you are planning to buy a fixer, do the work yourself and then move in, you are going to get a better loan than if you tell the lender you plan to buy, fix up and then sell.

The reasoning here, again, has to do with risk. Lenders feel that an owner-occupant who sees the property as shelter is far less likely to let that property go into foreclosure if times become difficult, than an investor who is looking only at the bottom line.

Thus, if you're an investor, you may find that an institutional lender such as a bank or a savings and loan will only give you a mortgage for a maximum of 70 percent of the appraised value of the property (70% LTV—Loan to Value). On the other hand, if you're going to be an owner-occupant, the lender may offer you a mortgage as high as 95 percent (95% LTV). This is a big reason that so many people who buy fixer properties make it a point to live in those properties as well.

---

*C*aution

Some people tell the lender they intend to do one thing and then do another. They may intend to move in, but then circumstances change and they sell instead.

While circumstances can certainly change, it's never a good idea to deceive a lender. For one thing, some are pretty savvy and have a good idea of what's going on. For another, the federal government investigates falsified loan applications and, given the huge increase in foreclosures during the recent real estate recession, has been prosecuting such cases aggressively.

Don't take a chance. Do the right thing. Tell the truth on your application. If you can move in, do so. It may mean getting a mortgage that will allow you to do the deal at an interest rate you can afford. But, if you can't move in, don't say you can. In the long run you'll get yourself into more trouble than it's worth.

So, how do you obtain 100 percent financing from an institutional lender? The answer is that you have to go about it differently.

Keep in mind that normally you really need two kinds of loans. You need a mortgage with which to buy the property initially. Then you also need a second mortgage or some other type of financing to handle the fix-up work itself. It is by combining these two types of financing that you can, sometimes, get institutional lenders to foot the entire bill.

Let's consider a different property that Lou purchased at a later time, a "rejuvenator" property. While it looked okay, cosmetically speaking, it was old and needed updating. It needed a new heating system, new plumbing and upgraded electrical. Lou felt that given the neighborhood and the climate, he also needed to add air-conditioning and put in a modern kitchen. Because of its obsolescence, Lou was able to get the seller to accept a very low offer. He felt that once he had upgraded the property, however, he could turn around and sell it for a substantial profit.

However, Lou needed a place to live himself. He was currently renting and, since the property was cosmetically okay, he figured he could move in and then, over time, upgrade the systems while he lived there.

Lou went to a local bank, one that offered mortgages for homes in that area. He asked the bank to design a special type of mortgage for him. First, it had to cover all or most of the purchase costs as possible. Then, it also had to cover the costs of fixing up the property.

The lender, who was flexible (as many local lenders are), agreed. What they gave Lou was a short-term construction loan, at a slightly higher interest rate than a standard permanent loan. A construction loan, as opposed to a permanent mortgage, pays out its funds in a number of installments, usually as work is done. For example, such a loan may have 5 payments or 10. You don't get the money until you do the

*C*aution

Building and Safety departments are usually willing to give an owner-occupant a permit to do almost any kind of work. You can get a permit to do gas, electrical, plumbing or whatever provided you are living in the property yourself. (Sometimes they ask that you continue to live in the home for period of time, perhaps 6 to 12 months.) On the other hand, they usually will not give you a permit to do this kind of work yourself if you're an absentee owner/investor. Rather, they will require that the work be done by licensed contractors—something to keep in mind.

work. Of course, you also don't pay interest on the money until you get it.

Under the construction loan, Lou would get a big payment that would initially help him purchase the house. Then he would get additional payments as he completed work on the property. The total loan amount (85 percent of value) was based not on the purchase price, but the estimated value of the property after the work was completed. What this meant was that the first payment covered almost the entire cost of purchasing the property while subsequent payments covered the fix-up costs. Since Lou had figured a 15 percent profit, the 85 percent mortgage covered almost everything. (Those things that his loan did not cover, he paid for out of advances on his credit card.)

No, you're not going to find every lender willing to give you a construction loan on a handyman's special. But there are some lenders who are willing to be creative. You may have to look hard, but it is possible.

Why Should You Pay Some Cash Out of Your Pocket?

We've seen two possible methods of getting 100 percent financing. However, I want to suggest that you *not* use them if at all possible. Rather, I feel it's better to get conventional financing by putting in as much as 20 percent of your own money.

I realize that this appears to fly in the face of the basic strategy that most people have about dealing in real estate; namely, use anybody's money but your own. However, there are definite advantages to using your own cash, some of which we touched on in Chapter 7.

The first is that you will make more money if you use your own money. You'll recall that in Lou's deal with Stan, the way he finally managed to secure 100 percent financing was by offering Stan a percentage of the profits.

But what if instead, he had simply bought Stan's property outright? What if he had come up with, say 30 percent, and had gotten a conventional mortgage from a lender who was willing to subordinate? (With 30 percent cash down, there are some high-risk lenders who will subordinate.)

Sure, it would have been a lot of money. But, on the other hand, he wouldn't have had to give Stan a percentage of the profits when it came time to sell. Upon sale, Lou would have gotten all of his own money back (from the buyer) plus all of the profits.

*H*int

One good reason to use your own money is that you don't have to give away pieces of the pie to get financing.

A second good reason for using some of your own cash is control. When Lou got a construction loan, he was taking the bank in as an overseer. The bank wanted to know everything about the job and how it was progressing. They wanted to see building department inspection sign-offs, paid receipts from labor and materials suppliers and photos of the construction itself. And then the bank was slow in cutting checks that Lou desperately needed to pay suppliers and laborers. The bank had no problem with holding checks up for days or even weeks at a time while an accountant mulled over the construction loan terms to be sure everything favored the bank.

Don't underestimate the problems that a controlling lender can dream up. Late payments, reduced amounts on checks, arguments—it's a can of worms you don't need when you're in the midst of fixing up a property.

If possible, I suggest using some of your own money. You'll make more profit in the long run and have fewer headaches while doing it.

Where Do You Get Handyman's Special Loans?

A lot depends on the type of loan you're looking for. If it's bare land (the hardest collateral to use), I suggest you only try a bank or private individual.

If it's a construction loan, a bank or possibly a savings and loan might do.

If it's a straight "permanent" mortgage, then you have at least the following sources (the actual names of these lenders can be found under the heading of "mortgages" in the phone book):

- Banks
- Savings and loans

- Mortgage brokers or bankers
- Commercial credit companies
- Credit unions (usually you must be a member)
- Sellers
- Private lenders

When Do You Seek Out a Private Lender?

Dealing with private lenders is an area that deserves a few paragraphs here. Private lenders are individuals (or sometimes corporations) who are willing to make high-risk loans for big rewards. Because of the terms they demand, most of us in real estate prefer not to use them unless absolutely necessary.

While a conventional lender may ask, for example, 8 percent interest, a private lender may want 16 percent. A conventional lender may want two points (a point is one percent of the loan amount) to make the loan; a private lender may want five points.

On the other hand, a conventional lender may not be willing to even consider you (because of spotty credit or the property selected). On the other hand, a private lender may take any and all properties. Most private lenders, however, will not lend more than 80 percent and frequently prefer to lend closer to 66 percent of the current appraised value.

Using a private lender, in my opinion, should only be done in times of absolute necessity—when you want the place, but you can't get financing anywhere else. If that's the case, then figure out the cost, make sure you can afford it and go for it. Better a tough lender, than none at all.

Finally, don't overlook the possibility of using your credit card or a personal line of credit for financing. (Some credit card companies as of this writing charge as little as 7 to 10 percent in interest.) A personal line of credit is an unsecured debt that some banks are willing to give to extremely credit-worthy customers.

However, be aware that you should arrange for both credit cards and lines of credit before you begin work or make the purchase. Once you're involved in a fix-up project, you may have other financing that will interfere with your ability to get new credit. (Remember: lenders don't like to give credit to anyone who they think may actually need it.) It's a good idea *before* applying for credit with a lender to do a credit check on yourself (almost any real estate agent can pull one and some credit companies will do it for a fee), then clear up any bad marks that appear. Also, call your employer and let him or her know that a credit company may be calling. Ask your employer to give you a good recommendation—most will. The same holds true for a landlord or other creditor you know personally.

How Do You Obtain a Mortgage?

The forms are often the same, regardless of where you apply. You fill out an application (usually a standard form that secondary lenders such as Fannie Mae or Freddie Mac accept). These are used almost industrywide. (If you're going to apply more than once, I suggest you make copies and save yourself a lot of hassle as you go along. Just fill in the information from the old form, or use it, when applying for the next loan.)

The lender will then obtain a credit report. You provide documentation of your income and bank balances. And the lender arranges to have the property appraised. If everything checks out, you get the mortgage. If it doesn't, you look elsewhere.

The procedure that lenders use to separate those who qualify from those who don't is quite complex to understand. It involves a rating system that gauges your ability to repay and your track record. It really isn't necessary to understand it. Just be aware that if you keep getting turned down for loans you think you ought to get, you may have a credit problem. (We'll get to that shortly.)

Should You Get a Fixed-Rate or Adjustable Rate Mortgage?

Thus far we've been talking about financing in general. However, as soon as you're out there looking for a loan you'll come up against the fixed-rate versus the adjustable rate mortgage (ARM) dilemma. Which is better for you?

To find out, you need to know some basics about both types. A fixed-rate mortgage is just that. Its interest rate does not vary during the life of the loan. For you, this means that you'll know exactly what your payment is month after month.

The adjustable rate mortgage is different because the interest rate adjusts periodically according to an index that is usually based on the costs of funds of one type or another. With an ARM, you never know what your payments are going to be.

On the other hand, ARMs offer something that is of potentially great advantage to handyman's special investors: a lower-than-market initial interest rate (sometimes also called a "teaser"). If you only plan to keep the property a short time and then resell, why not get a mortgage with a low initial interest rate? (The danger with this is, of course, that you won't be able to sell and will be stuck with the property after the teaser wears off.)

Let's consider ARMs more closely. ARMs benefit the lender more than the borrower, since the interest rate can move up or down depending on market conditions. Therefore, given a choice between an ARM and a fixed-rate mortgage, most lenders would favor the ARM while most borrowers would prefer the fixed rate. For this reason, lenders have to sweeten the pot in order to get borrowers to go for ARMs. They do this with the "teaser," a below-market initial rate that gets you hooked on the mortgage. Once you've gotten the loan, then the rate moves up until it's at par with the market. Get that teaser and then, when the lender begins to crank up the interest rate, sell the property. Many people do it. It's perfectly legal. But, don't get caught not being able to resell.

Steps of ARMs

If you go for an ARM with a teaser, carefully check out the "steps" and the adjustment periods. ARMs all have limitations on the maximum amount that the interest rate can move up or down in any given period. The interest rate movement is called the step. For example, an ARM may have steps of 1 percent. This means that in each adjustment period, the interest rate can vary up or down a maximum of 1 percent. The time between each step is called the adjustment period.

Adjustment Periods

When getting an ARM, what you ideally want is a mortgage with very low steps and very long adjustment periods. I suggest never getting larger than 1 percent steps. If possible, get ¾ percent or ½ percent maximum steps. At the same time, get adjustment periods that are long, hopefully six months or longer. Unfortunately, many ARMS adjust monthly!

Here are some other basic features of an ARM that you should be aware of.

Index

This is what the interest rate is tied to. It could be anything from T-bill yields, to the 11th federal reserve district cost of funds, to the LIBOR (London Interbranch Borrowing Rate). You want an index that isn't going to shoot up quickly, thus taking your interest rate with it.

Margin

The margin is the difference between the index and the interest rate you are charged. You want a fair margin, one that brings the interest rate up to market, not higher than market.

Negative Amortization

Some mortgages have a "cap" or maximum amount that the payment rises each adjustment period. The problem is that there is usually no cap on the interest rate. The result is that interest due but not paid on the mortgage is added to the principal. You can end up owing more than you borrowed! Stay away from this type of mortgage as though it were the plague.

What Are Other Types of Financing I Can Use?

Here are some borrowing alternatives:

Assumptions

Some older mortgages can be assumed or taken over. The advantage is that you get the old interest rate and terms. Basically, we're talking about two types of assumable loans today. The first type is government guaranteed or insured loans, such as VA and FHA mortgages. The second is ARMs, most of which are assumable, but only if you qualify at the current market rate.

VA and FHA loans are no longer freely assumable, as they were in the past. Depending on when they were placed on the property, you may need to submit an application and credit report to assume them.

The advantage of an assumption is the reduced cost. An old FHA or VA loan may have a much lower interest rate. This makes it a good assumption possibility. The problem is that usually an older loan is written for substantially less than the purchase price. In other words, it isn't a big enough mortgage. Thus, in addition to an assumption, you also may need to get a second, new mortgage either from an institution or the seller to get to the total amount you need to borrow.

Note: ARMs are usually assumable and may have large enough balances to be worthwhile, because they are usually fairly recent loans. However, with an ARM you get the current market rate and you have to qualify fully. The advantage, however, is that the cost of getting the loan, points, title insurance, etc., is usually greatly reduced. Thus, there might be some cost advantage in assuming an ARM as well.

Second Mortgages

These are mortgages that institutional lenders and sellers often give when there's already a first mortgage on the property that you're buying. The term varies with second mortgages, although institutional seconds are typically for 5 to 15 years. They may either be fixed rate or ARMs.

If you get this loan after you've bought the property, they are commonly called Home Equity loans and the money can be used for almost any purpose. But, you must have sufficient equity in the property in order to get this type of loan. Usually lenders are hesitant to give a home equity loan until at least six months have passed since the owner purchased the property. However, if you can demonstrate that you have the equity (either you put a lot of money down or the property has significantly appreciated in value), you can often get this type of loan.

For more information on real estate financing, I suggest you check into my *Tips and Traps When Mortgage Hunting* (McGraw-Hill, 1991).

Can You Work Out Credit Problems?

There are many books on the market that purport to tell you how to eliminate credit problems. The truth doesn't take a book to fill. If you have a credit problem you have only two options: either you have to find a way to get the blemish removed from your credit, or you must find a lender who is willing to ignore the blemish and still give you a mortgage. Here are some hints in both areas.

Helping Bad Credit Reports

Generally speaking, the only way you can get a bad report removed from your credit history is to have the source call or write the credit reporting agency and tell them to take it off. Why would they do that? They may have made a mistake. Mistakes in credit reporting are legend. You could have paid the bill and the payment might not have been noted. Or the bad credit report could be for someone else. Be sure you correct an error as it can continue to come back and haunt you.

If you can't get the bad report removed by the source for whatever reason, at least insist that the credit reporting agency include a letter of explanation from you. Often you are allowed to have such a letter noted. Be sure you explain what the extenuating circumstances are.

Helping Wary Lenders

If you know your lender is going to get a bad credit report on you, take the bull by the horns and deal with it up front. I had a friend who had terrible credit. It came about because she was living with a fellow who used and then abused her credit. He charged all sorts of things on her credit and never paid for them. When she found out about it, they had a fight and he left. But by that time, she was obligated but had not a chance in the world of being able to pay off the large amounts.

When she applied for a mortgage, she included a letter of explanation, noting that this had all occurred some three years earlier and that prior to that time and since it, she had perfect credit. The first lender she went to turned her down. But the second accepted the explanation and moved forward on the mortgage.

Can You Get Other People To Put Up Capital?

Finally, there's the matter of getting someone else to put up the capital you need for your fixer project. Is this done often? Yes, I believe it is. Who usually puts up the money? Usually it's close family members.

---

*C*aution

Lenders are like elephants: they never forget bad credit. At all costs, try to avoid late payments on a mortgage or the ultimate worst, a foreclosure. Lenders hate lending money to anyone who hasn't kept up their mortgage, no matter the reason.

Quite frankly, your best chance of getting the money you need with nothing more than a handshake is from your parents, siblings or other close relatives. Assuming that over the years you've convinced them of your financial acumen and your strong feelings of responsibility toward repaying a debt, they may be more than happy to give you a personal loan.

Quite frankly, I believe close friends are the least likely to lend you money. They may be competitive with you, jealous of your accomplishments or scornful of your failures. You can try, but don't be surprised if you come up empty-handed.

Then, of course, there are associates. Members of your dream team, co-workers, people you may know socially (but are not close friends with), may be willing to put up the capital you need. But to get it they are likely to want a piece of the action. Indeed, your best chance of getting them to put up money is to present the deal as an investment opportunity. Present it as a straight loan and, I believe, you're less likely to get the money.

Finally, there are venture capitalists who make a business of lending money to small and large businesses. However, to attract these people you will probably need to borrow a large sum and will need a written proposal or plan. Venture capitalists are a world unto their own and I don't suggest you consider them until you have a million-dollar minimum project, a strong track record of success and a business plan that simply cannot be denied.

As we noted at the beginning of this chapter, financing is the name of the game in real estate. Those who get it have the opportunity to move forward with purchases and with fixing up property. Those who can't secure financing are often left out of the handyman's specials playing field.

My suggestion is that you pay special attention to financing your deal. Don't think of financing as something extra, like fries on the side of a hamburger. The financing is the meat inside the bun. Without it there is no burger and no deal!

Get your financing early. Get enough of it to do the whole deal from start to finish. But don't get buried by an overwhelming interest rate or too-high costs for your financing.

CHAPTER 9

Collaborating with the Seller

Have you ever gone looking for a fixer and found a great property, only to discover the seller is unreasonable about the price? Yes, she wants to sell. But she's convinced that the property is worth far more, even in its present condition, than you're willing and able to offer.

If you've spent any time at all looking for fixers, I'm sure you've run into this situation. If you have, then you've probably done what I and most others do. Chalk it up to experience and keep looking.

Sometimes, however, there's an alternative that can work with an intransigent seller: making them a partner. In Chapter 8, we introduced the idea of partnership in order to get financing. Now, we're going to expand it into something more formal. Remember, sometimes sellers can only come to terms with what their property is worth when they actually see what has to be done, see the work being done and then realize the costs involved. There's nothing more convincing than actually doing the fix-up work.

Of course, most times sellers don't want to be bothered with this. They just want a clean sale. They want to get their money out of the property so they can move on and leave the headaches to you. However, other times sellers simply can't sell this way and in those cases, they may be willing to listen to reason.

A Shared Fixer?

Sam had a two-story Victorian house in San Francisco. The building was 80 years old and needed both cosmetic work as well as rejuvenation. The exterior needed new sheathing and a roof; the inside needed plastering and restaining of the extensive woodwork. A new heating system and work on the drains, as well as revamped baths and kitchen were also in order. The work was extensive and, as Alice, who wanted to buy and fix the place up realized, expensive. She calculated it would cost close to $150,000 to fix up the property and get her profit out of it. (Fixers of this magnitude are not unusual in San Francisco where housing prices are among the highest in the nation.) Sam, however, was stuck on asking a price that was only $80,000 less than what the house would sell for if it were completely refurbished. There was a $70,000 difference between what Alice was offering and what Sam was willing to sell for; they were a veritable ocean apart.

When Alice talked with Sam, however, she quickly learned that she wasn't the first person to differ with him on this. He had had the house on the market for over a year and numerous other investors had come by, wanting to fix it up. All of their estimates had been in about the same ballpark. It was just that Sam was stubborn.

So Alice gave him this proposal: Why not work with her to fix up the property and then sell it when it was refurbished? A completed fixer in the neighborhood should be a cinch to sell. That way Sam would know exactly how much it cost to fix up the place and how much it would ultimately sell for. He could share in the profits.

Sam thought it was the best idea since sliced bread. He jumped at the chance of doing it. Alice told him, "Whoa, we have to set up the ground rules so that neither of us gets hurt on the deal." Here's what Alice proposed.

1. Sam would share ownership of the property with Alice.

2. Alice would secure added financing to do the fix-up work and see that it was all done properly.

3. After the work was done, they would call in a professional appraiser to tell them what it was worth and they would list it for that amount.

4. When the place was sold, Alice would take 10 percent of the sales price as her share of the profit. Out of the balance, all costs of the sale (including the commission) as well as the mortgages on the property would be paid. What was left would be Sam's share.

For Alice, it was a very sweet deal. To begin, she wouldn't have to come up with any down payment or arrange any purchase money financing. She was simply getting half ownership in the property directly from Sam.

Of course, she would be responsible for getting financing to do the work and getting it done right. Sam insisted on a clause specifying that if she backed out on this, the ownership would immediately revert back to him alone.

Finally, Alice's profit was almost guaranteed, as long as the house eventually sold. She figured it would sell in the $500,000 to $600,000 range, which meant she'd make

$50,000 to $60,000 on the deal. Probably less than if she bought it outright herself, but then again she didn't have to come up with any cash.

For Sam, it didn't sound like such a bad deal either. He was wary of the 10 percent profit to Alice, but agreed that she had to do a lot of work to get it, so it was probably fair. Further, he would watch closely to see that no more money was spent on the fix-up than absolutely necessary. As a result, his remainder would be:

Sam's Share

Sales Price
Less Costs of Sale
Less Payoff of Mortgages
Less Alice's 10 percent

Sam was sure that his profit would be more than if he had sold it for what Alice offered in the first place. (As it ultimately turned out, it was just a tiny bit more.)

Keep in mind that all this worked out in large part because Sam had a big equity in the house. He could afford to be flexible about what he received because he didn't have a big mortgage hanging over his head. This sort of deal won't work when the seller just has marginal equity.

Understanding Equity Sharing

The technique used in Sam and Alice's deal is called "equity sharing." It's a concept that came into existence in the late 1970s, although for a different purpose. Back then, property was rapidly appreciating in all parts of the country. If you bought, you could assume that your home would go up in value a minimum of 5 percent a year. In some cases, that figure was 10 percent a year or higher!

The problem was that then, as now, those who wanted to buy frequently couldn't afford to. They didn't have enough money for the down payment. On the other hand, sellers looking at the rapid price appreciation were not so anxious to sell. They kept wondering to themselves about holding on to the property. Why sell something that was going up so rapidly in price? One answer was equity sharing.

Back then, the way it worked was that a buyer and seller would enter into an equity sharing agreement. While the terms could vary enormously, generally they provided that the seller would throw in his equity and the buyer would move into the property, make the monthly payments for mortgage, taxes and insurance and maintain the place. Then, after a set period of time, typically a few years, the property would be placed on the market.

From the sale, the seller would get back his equity. Any balance (and there was usually a big balance given the price appreciation) would be split between the equity sharers. Many such arrangements were made and, while some didn't work out, many did with both parties coming out handsomely.

While the terms are certainly different, it is possible to equity-share a fixer. You're the investor in this case, the party coming in who wants to buy the property. The seller is the one who shares. On the next page are three reasons why you would want to equity-share a fixer.

If it turns out that any of the above reasons fit you, then you should at least consider the possibility of doing an equity-share with the seller. In order to do this, however, you'll have to sell the owner of the property on the concept. To do that you must demonstrate at least three qualities.

Reasons for Sharing Equity

1. The seller is unrealistic about the sales price in unrefurbished condition (as in our example).

2. You don't have the cash to buy the fixer outright.

3. You can't get the financing to buy the fixer outright.

Selling the Owner on Equity Sharing

1. **Be Honest.** You need to convince an owner/seller that you are completely honest. Sellers must believe that you will do what you say and not cheat them along the way, or they will never go along with whatever you propose.

   How do you convince another person of your honesty? It's simple: Never exaggerate and never equivocate. When there's a problem or something comes up to your disadvantage, admit it. People judge us by how well we respond to adversity. If it turns out we were wrong in an honest mistake, do we admit it? If something occurs that could cost us money, do we try to hide the fact or bring it out in the open?

   I personally like to go out for lunch or coffee with a person with whom I'm going to work and just talk. We don't have to talk about anything in particular. But while we're talking I listen carefully to what the other person says and judge their level of honesty. I might bring up a point that's disadvantageous (on the surface) for them. How do they handle it? Do they hide it? Ignore it? Or acknowledge it?

If you're up front with sellers and they are reasonable (something that's essential for the sharing arrangement), they should be able to sense your honesty pretty quickly and it won't be a problem.

2. Explain Everything. It's important that sellers understand what's involved in a shared equity arrangement, both the good and the bad. Your partner needs to know up front what will happen if things go well and what will happen if they go badly. In order to make an informed decision, both the risks and rewards have to be clearly outlined.

    You also need to demonstrate that you are capable of handling the fix-up work. I don't encourage you to try sharing equity if this is your first fixer. Rather, you need a successful track record to help convince a seller to go along with a shared equity proposal. Ideally, you should be able to point to half a dozen other properties you fixed up and sold for a profit. Or at least a few. This helps establish your credibility in a seller's eyes.

3. Show the Advantages. Finally, understand why sellers want to get rid of their properties and point out why doing a shared equity could be to their advantage. In our example with Sam and Alice, it turned out that Sam did not make significantly more money. However, in other situations, particularly when the fixer is in such run-down condition that a sale at almost any price is difficult, it could work out much better.

In short, you must present sharing equity as an attractive alternative. If the owner/seller agrees (and has sufficient equity), you're on your way.

How Do You Protect Yourself?

In order to be successful, however, you have to be sure that you are protected.

$\mathcal{C}$aution

Taking in a partner in *any* transaction is always risky business. You can't know that your partner will be as honest or as savvy as you. Your partner may try to cheat you or do something foolish that could cost you money. Therefore, you need to protect yourself as much as possible.

While there is no such thing as absolute protection, you can get assurance that you'll be okay in the deal by making all the terms very clear to everyone, including having a written agreement. Here's what I would consider *the absolute minimum* in any shared equity agreement I signed. (You may want or need additional terms.)

11 Requirements To Share Equity

1. Written Agreement—This should be prepared by an attorney who is familiar with the concept and has done these before. Some real estate attorneys have ready-to-go forms that they can adjust to fit your specific situation. Don't attempt to create an equity sharing agreement without an attorney's help.

2. Ownership—You must clearly spell out how the title to the property is going to be held during the fix-up period. Ideally, you would share title with the seller. However, in order to keep the current financing, it may be to everyone's advantage to have the seller keep title with you having a contract. If that's the case, be sure that you are protected from the owner selling out from under you to someone else. You might, for example, have all additional financing in the owner's name, that way you wouldn't be liable for it. Or you may be able to have something recorded that protects your interest and prevents sale without your approval.

3. Time Frame—You need to be very specific about how long you will have to do the fix-up work (allow yourself ample time) and when the house will be put up for sale. You don't want a situation where the owner keeps procrastinating about selling the property after it's fully fixed.

4. Work To Be Done—Be very clear about what fix-up work you plan to do, how you plan to do it, where the money is coming from (additional financing) and how long you will take. The seller needs to know these things in order to feel comfortable about the deal.

5. Profits—Be very clear about the profits. In our last example, Alice's profits came off the top. In other deals you may make, the seller may want to get his equity out, pay all costs and then divide the remainder. Be sure to strike a deal that you feel is fair to you.

6. Appraisal—The value of the property at resale is critical. Be sure you're in agreement on some method for determining what the resale price will be. For example, you could hire an independent appraiser, or you could call in three real estate agents for their evaluation and then take an average of the three. You should also specify that the price will be reduced by a certain amount every three months (or whatever term), if the property doesn't sell.

7. Sale—You need to specify how the property will be resold. Are you going to do it FSBO? If so, it could take longer. Are you going to list it? With whom?

8. Maintenance Costs—Someone's going to have to pay for the mortgage, taxes, insurance and upkeep until the property resells. Who is that going to be? If it's you, how will you get your money back? If it's the owner, are the amounts to be added to his equity (which may come out of the deal first), or are these amounts to be considered as costs of doing the deal?

9. Occupancy—Does the owner get to stay in the property while the work is being done? Do you? Are you going to rent it out? What about those times when the occupant must temporarily leave in order for some fix-up work to be completed?

10. Decision Not To Sell—What if one party doesn't want to sell? Agreements are great. But you or your partner's frame of mind when it's time to sell can be far different from when you entered into the agreement. What if the seller decides that rather than sell, the place came out so beautifully he'd like to live in it himself? Or he'd like to hold it as an investment rental? Your agreement should include detailed information on how one partner can buy out the other, including costs.

11. Arbitration—Finally, there's always the chance that you forgot to include something or that somewhere along the way a disagreement will arise. How are you going to deal with it? There's always the matter of court and lawyers. However, a more reasonable and less expensive approach may be arbitration. You and your partner may want to agree to arbitration in advance. However, if you do, be sure to specify how you will determine who will arbitrate. You may want to use a professional arbitrator, but be aware that that solution tends to be quite costly.

CHAPTER 10

Buying Apartment and Commercial Fixers

Handyman's special opportunities abound in areas other than houses. For example, in today's market there are numerous apartment and commercial fixers just waiting for TLC to turn them into winners. If you're looking for more than the ordinary challenge, you may want to consider these.

Apartment Fixers

From about the late 1960s to the late 1980s, apartment buildings in many areas of the country simply kept going up in price. One reason for this was the general inflation in real estate values. Another was that it was possible to keep raising rents and as long as rents went up, building valuations (which are based on income) went up as well. Finally, in some cases apartments were sold, fixed up and then resold as condos. These were called "conversions."

Since the late 1980s, however, prices for apartment buildings have leveled off or, in many areas, declined along with
the nationwide slump in real estate. However, this slump is
currently ending in many areas, providing an opportunity for
investors. Also, during the recent slump, many apartment
buildings were "let go." The owners did little-to-no maintenance, meaning that today they are in bad shape, often with
many vacancies and lower-than-expected rents.

For the enterprising individual, the challenge is to find one
of these, buy it, fill it with high-paying tenants and sell for
amazingly high profits. It's being done, today, and you can
do it too.

How Do You Buy an Apartment Fixer?

In Chapter 3, we discussed where to find these buildings
and what to look for. Here, we'll talk about how to buy them.

What you need to do, as with a fixer house, is determine
two values: (1) the ultimate value that property will bring on
resale after it's fixed up, and (2) the value you need to place
on it now in order to be able to buy, fix up and sell it for a
profit. Generally speaking, the way that you accomplish this
is to first determine the ultimate value and then determine
your costs. (We'll see how to do this in the next section.)
Then subtract your costs and your anticipated profit from the
ultimate value, and you have the maximum amount you can
afford to offer.

In addition to the rules for making low-ball offers that
we've already discussed (Chapter 6) and structuring the deal
(Chapter 7), there are some special considerations you will
want to keep in mind when buying apartment buildings.

Special Considerations

True Rental Rate As noted, value is based on rental income. A multiplier is often used; for example, the value may be 10 times the annual rental rate. If you have five units that each rents at $500 per month, you have $30,000 a year income and a rough value of $300,000. What should be obvious is that you can't know how much the true value is until you know what the true rental rate is.

So spend some time finding out. Don't just ask for the rental income of the units you're buying. Chances are there are other similar units around. Check with their owners (or tenants) see how much they're bringing in. Find out the true rental rate. If you don't know what amount of annual rental income to expect from it, you'll never get an accurate price for the property.

True Vacancy Rate Similarly, every area has a vacancy rate. Find out what that is for the building you are considering buying.

Don't accept an owner's estimation that, "We figure about 5 percent for vacancies," or "The property is never vacant—it rents up right away."

Again, check with surrounding apartment owners of similar buildings. Most will be happy to tell you their vacancy rate. Also, find out if there's an apartment owner's association in the area. They may have some hard figures as well.

Finally, don't forget the time between rentals that it takes to clean up a unit. (This is not the same as fixing up the building. We're talking here of cleaning up after an old tenant moves out and before a new one can move in.) Some apartment owners have a turnaround time of one day; others take a month. Sometimes it depends on the size of the units and how new they are. (Is the carpeting new and easily cleanable? What about the appliances?)

Rent Control Restrictions   Nothing will sink you faster than to learn, after a purchase, that the area still has rental controls. These are set by local governments and essentially mean that you can't raise a tenant's rent except by a set (usually menial) amount. Check this out with the local government (usually a rent control board or sometimes a building and planning department).

Keep in mind that sometimes even in areas with rent control, when a tenant voluntarily moves out, the landlord may be allowed to raise the rent, even up to current market levels. Also, some allowance may be made when the building is sold.

Cleaning/Security Deposits   Find out who has these and how much they are. You don't want to buy an apartment building only to learn that the former owner kept thousands of dollars in deposits that tenants now expect you to return.

The location, amount and disposition of deposits should be clearly spelled out in a written purchase agreement. (Sometimes the deposits will be so high they can be a deal maker or deal breaker.)

If you're new to apartment ownership, you will find that there are many other questions. We'll deal with some of these in the next section. But, in any event, you would be wise to consult with a savvy real estate agent in your area who deals strictly with these units. This agent can usually tell you more in a few minutes than you could learn in months of investigating this area for yourself.

Commercial Fixers

These follow a similar pattern to apartment buildings. They were hot until the late 1980s and have since cooled considerably. Before buying, you should carefully check your area to see if it still has a large surplus of commercial space available. If it does, you may want to pass. You simply aren't going to be able to sell for much of a profit in the immediate future if there's lots of similar property on the market. Further, you will also have trouble renting.

The Importance of Location

It's been said many times that location is the most important factor in real estate value. When it comes to *commercial* real estate, location becomes almost the *only* factor. It doesn't matter whether it's a small strip shopping center, a large mall-type center or office space—what will most determine success or failure is location.

Fortunately, today there are properties with reasonably good locations that are still available at low prices. (Most of the really terrific locations, of course, are still quoting high prices.) Consequently, if you're interested in fixing up commercial real estate, the first thing that you need to do is to find run-down properties in great locations. (Check back into Chapters 3 and 4 for clues on how to do this.) In addition, contact commercial real estate agents. In larger real estate offices, there are typically one or two agents who specialize in commercial properties. (Everyone else sells houses.) You need to contact these special agents.

When trying to evaluate the location for a commercial fixer, you need to look at this a bit differently than for residential property. What you should pay special attention to is "exposure." By this, I mean you need a good location on a heavily trafficked street. If it's office space, a good commercial location doesn't hurt. But being isolated on a side street (a killer for purely commercial) isn't always so bad for offices, if there is ample parking.

Also pay special attention to the surrounding neighborhood, particularly with small strip malls. (With a large building or mall, the commercial property, in essence, creates its own neighborhood environment. For a mall owner, the biggest concern often is being close to freeway off-ramps.) With small strip shops or office buildings, however, you want to be near other similar businesses so that the combined effect is to bring in more customers. Of course, there's also a downside. Today, many older commercial and office buildings are in deteriorating neighborhoods with crime problems. The personal safety aspect could drive customers and tenants away. I never buy anything in a neighborhood where I'm afraid to walk in the evening.

You also need to be sure the commercial building has easy access from the street, so customers can get in and that it has adequate parking. Finally there's the matter of how the property looks to someone approaching it. It has to have basically a nice appeal, or you may need to put up a new front facade as part of your fixing up.

How Do You Get the Right Price?

Just as with other property, you need to know your costs before you can whittle down to the price you can offer. However, unlike with residential property, commercial property often has a design factor. It has to look appealing to draw people in. Therefore, as part of determining your costs, you should consult with a good architect (perhaps a member of your "dream team"?) who can turn you on to different ways to spice up the building.

Also, just as with apartment buildings, you want to get a good handle on how much you can reasonably expect for rents and what the vacancy rate is. Keep in mind that the rental and vacancy rates are often affected by the overall amount of space available. If there's too much space available, landlords cut their rental rates to attract tenants. Thus, you can have no vacancies at a low rate or very high vacancies at a higher rental rate. You need to know what you're likely to experience in your area at the present time.

Special Considerations

Just as with apartment buildings, there are things to watch out for that are peculiar to commercial buildings. Here are a few to check out:

Lease Terms   Check the leases of the current tenants. Commercial leases are significantly different from residential leases. With the commercial property, you often want the tenant to pay not only the rent, but the utilities and sometimes even the taxes and the insurance. "Net, net, net" leases are commonly used in these situations.

Some leases also provide that the rent is a minimum based on the gross (or net) sales of the tenant. As those sales increase, you get a percentage of them. These are typically found in large commercial developments.

Finally, you want to know the length of the lease. If the building is only half full, but those tenants have low-paying, long-term leases, you may want to pass. You could fix up the building and still not be able to raise rents and resell for a profit. (Like apartment buildings, the value of commercial buildings is largely determined by income.)

Perks   In commercial buildings, tenants will sometimes have perks. These could be certain reserved parking spots, the ability to use a walkway for tables (as is the case with some restaurants) or having the tenant's name on a big sign facing the street. Sometimes these perks are understandable and reasonable. Other times, they inhibit your ability to fix up or even resell. You may have to check with each tenant separately to find what the perks are.

3. Fix-Up Restrictions Thus far, we've assumed that there would be no barriers to your fixing up a property. Usually there aren't. However, that can change significantly when it comes to commercial property.

I was once involved with a fairly large community shopping center that was nearly 30 years old. It was run down and many of the stores were vacant, but it was in a great area with lots of parking and easy access. It was a perfect fixer. Or so I thought!

Then I learned that the city had passed resolutions requiring that if any major work was done to a commercial center, it had to be brought up to current city code for that type of building. No sweat? You'd bring it up to code anyhow?

The problem is, they weren't just talking about things like electrical and plumbing. They were also talking about building design and landscaping. The current code called for no signs facing the street—the "kiss of death" to many businesses.

The buildings would also have to be converted to a Spanish rustic architecture, then in vogue in the area. And a greenbelt, or grass strip, would have to be added between the sidewalk and the buildings, requiring major reconstruction work.

In short, it would have cost millions to bring the shopping center up to current code, more than the seller wanted as his asking price! Needless to say, I passed on the deal.

Be sure to check out any local government restrictions and regulations affecting a commercial center you may be interested in. You may get a shock.

Toxic Sites You wouldn't buy a toxic site, you say? What if you didn't know it was toxic?

These days toxic sites aren't what they always appear to be. What if there were once a gas station on the land? Even though the station may be years gone, the tanks (or spillage from the tanks) may still be on or under the ground. Put your name on the deed and you could end up responsible for the entire clean up, which could cost thousands or hundreds of thousands of dollars or more.

What if there was a small auto-supply store in the strip center you're considering? What if they dumped old oil and battery acid on the ground out back? Who do you think will be responsible for hauling yards of dirt to a toxic dump site?

We're living in an era when we are increasingly conscious of protecting the environment around us, which is, of course, a great concept. We all want to breathe clean air and have healthy soil. But, you'll get a whole new perspective on it if you unwittingly are asked to pay for someone else's earlier environmental mistakes.

Weather Associated Problems   In some areas of the country, the weather can be a factor in both the rental income and the aging of a property. In Phoenix, for example, don't expect to do a land office business in summer. When the weather is 115 degrees in the shade, people don't go out as much during the day and only into air-conditioned buildings in the evening. If you planned on a year-round business and don't have air-conditioning, you could be in trouble.

Similarly, some areas in "mountain country" simply close up for three months, typically December, January and February. The weather's too cold and blizzardy to do any real business. If you buy in the summer and don't know about the winter, you also could be in trouble.

Apartment and commercial buildings offer rare fixer opportunities at the present time. Many are well priced and within the range of investors. Further, as the real estate market gets better in many areas of this country, these properties stand to offer really impressive profits to buyers.

If you want a challenge beyond the single-family house fixer, look to an apartment building or even a small strip mall. The risks are usually greater, but so are the rewards.

CHAPTER 11

Guesstimating Fix-Up Costs

You need to know in advance—and pretty darn accurately—how much it's going to cost you to fix up a house or any other property. If you don't know your expenses, it's impossible to work back to figure out what you should pay. And if you pay too much, then you'll lose money when it comes time to sell. (Even if you intend to live in the property for a period of time, you should make your calculations as if you were going to sell immediately, or else you could build in a loss.)

Knowing how much your expenses are going to be in advance, however, is only partly science. There's also a good measure of judgment, experience and even luck involved. As a result, your best guess is in reality only a "guesstimate"—an estimate of what you think (hope) your true costs will be. In this chapter, we're going to see how to make that guesstimate as accurate as possible.

Is It Really That Complicated?

I worked with a fellow some years ago who had a mind built like a calculator. Philip would take into account all our costs as well as all our income and would know at any given time our cash flow as well as our profit/loss. He even played a game with our accountant who did the books at the end of the year. The day the accountant came in, Philip would write down on a piece of paper his guess at the profit for that year, seal it in an envelope and hand it to the accountant. The accountant would then work days on the books to come up with the true profit figure. When the work was done, the envelope was opened. Philip was never more than a hundred dollars off!

Most of us, however, don't think like Philip. Indeed, I sometimes have trouble remembering a phone number I just heard, let alone the price of 17 gallons of paint or how much a drywall laborer wants for three walls.

It's not just a matter of writing it down. It's also application. Many of the prices and costs you will need to handle will be for future work. While it's fairly easy to keep track of expenses that you've already incurred (in a worst case, you simply stick the invoices in a shoebox and they're there later on when the accountant comes in), it's a different ball game with estimates.

Estimates not only need to be written down, but evaluated. You may get three or more estimates for a particular task. You may get separate estimates for labor and for materials. Different people will want to do the work differently. Hence, comparing estimates may be like comparing apples and oranges. And finally, there's the matter of whether you will hire someone to do the work or you'll end up doing it yourself and what that will do to the cost figures.

Trying to keep track of all this in your head, even for a small fix-up job like a kitchen or bath, will not only give you a headache, but probably will result in costly errors. Therefore, no matter how big or how small the job, no matter whether you're just going to paint a few rooms or rebuild an entire house, I always suggest you use an estimator's sheet.

Should You Use a Guesstimator's Sheet?

There's nothing magical about an estimator's sheet (actually a "guesstimator" sheet). You can easily create one yourself specifically for the job you have. You can borrow one from builders, who often have designed their own. You can pick them up in larger stationery stores. Or you can use the one I've included as Figure 11.1 at the end of this chapter.

The point, however, is that you learn how to properly use such a sheet. If you do, it will save you a whole bunch of time and money.

While our estimator's sheet is fairly self-explanatory and the basic method for using it is quite simple, the application is a bit trickier and there are some areas that deserve special attention, especially if this is all new to you. Let's take an example.

Jim and Mary are considering buying a handyman's special. Their goal is to get into a particular high-priced neighborhood and their only option, because of limited funds and income, is a fixer. So they are looking at all the run-down houses they can find in that one neighborhood.

For most people, the typical method of checking out a house is to wander through the rooms as an agent points out this or that. This method is fine for first scouting out property. But, once you identify a likely prospect as a fixer and before you make an offer, you need to go back and fill out a guesstimate sheet.

Jim and Mary identified two likely candidates. So they went back to each, accompanied by an agent in one case and an owner in the other. They explained that they were thinking of fixing up the property, if they bought it. What they were doing now was taking an hour or two to get an estimate of what it would cost to do the work.

---

*H*int

The minute you bring out your guesstimate sheet at a fixer, chances are the owner or the agent will tell you that they've already had a builder give an estimate and it's for $$$. Never mind what they say . . . do the estimating yourself. At this stage, someone else's estimate may be interesting, but you need to know what it's going to cost *you* to do the work, not them.

Jim and Mary carefully identified each problem with the property that required fix-up. Once identified, they used their guesstimate sheet to come up with a cost to fix all the problems.

Of course, in the majority of cases, they didn't know the true cost, so they put down their estimate of what work and materials would be required and put a question mark where the price should go, to be filled in later.

Bring a Camera?

Jim and Mary also brought a camera along. It's important to remember that while work to be done may seem perfectly clear when it's right in front of us, when we leave and then think about it, we may confuse one room with another, work that needs to be done to the bathroom sink with that which needs to be done in the kitchen, and so forth.

So Mary brought a camera along. No, she didn't photograph everything that needed to be done in the house. They knew that a complete painting inside and out was necessary, so there was no need to photograph the walls. But, she did take pictures of the shower stall in one bathroom and the tub in another, both of which would require fixing. Likewise, she took a picture of some holes in the outside wall and the kitchen sink. These would prove helpful later on when she and Jim tried to get more specific cost estimates.

Finally, when they had noted everything they could and had taken pictures of anything that they might forget (or which could be confusing upon reflection), they left the house. Their next task was to nail down accurate prices. We'll cover that shortly, but first, let's consider whether their guesstimate sheet was all inclusive.

How To Ensure You Are Including All Possible Fix-Up Work

Every job is different. You may go into a house and discover that what needs to be done is fixing hardwood floors. Some boards have dry rot. Others have termite damage. Parts of the floor will need to be pried up and replaced. Some underneath supports may need work. Then there's sanding, priming, varnishing and whatever else may be needed.

Does your guesstimate sheet cover everything that needs to be done for flooring? Do you have categories for:

- Removal of damaged wood
- Replacing flooring
- Bracing supports

- Nailing and filling nail holes
- Sanding
- Priming and varnishing

If you're using a standard form, even the one presented at the end of this chapter, the appropriate categories aren't always going to be there. As a result, you need to be able to add categories to fit the job.

Hint

Never make the job fit your guesstimate form. If you do, chances are some expense will be left out or underestimated. Add to the categories on your guesstimate sheet as you go.

Further, in addition to the flooring, your fixer may require replastering walls, rehabilitating an old furnace, refurbishing stained glass windows, painting and landscaping. While most of these general categories may indeed be on your sheet, others may not. You need to be able to not only add specifics, but add categories as well.

Are the Price Estimates Realistic?

The whole idea behind a guesstimate sheet is that you determine what it's going to cost to do a particular job. However, as noted earlier, you really may have no idea what it's going to cost. This is particularly the case if you're new to the game. So what do you do now?

What you need to do is research. You need to spend some time, perhaps a day or two, finding out what things cost. This may involve making calls to tradespeople to find out how much they charge for particular work, by the hour and by the job. It may mean making appointments with them to go and look at the property. And it certainly will mean getting up-to-speed on what materials cost.

Finding Out Hourly Costs

You may need a plumber, an electrician, a painter, a person to install drywall, another person to handle taping and texturing of drywall and so on. You will probably want to know how much these people charge to do the work. How do you find out?

It's simple. You call them. In earlier chapters, we described creating a dream team. We also talked about networking with tradespeople. Both of these techniques will help you to quickly find out about costs. However, they are for after you've gotten going. When you're first starting out, you're going to have to pick up the phone book and make some calls. You should very quickly get the answers you need.

By the way, you can often get these answers right over the phone. While I've never had a tradesperson not tell me that they needed to see the job to give any sort of accurate estimate, I've also never had them fail to tell me what they would charge *in general* for the job, as long as I preface my question by first saying something such as, "All I want is a ballpark figure. I'm not going to hold you to it. I just want to know in general."

Getting Job Estimates

On the other hand, particularly if this is all new to you, you may not have any idea of what really needs to be done. Yes, the bathroom is a mess. The tub has deep scratches and gouges in it. There's a crack in the sink. One cabinet door is off. But must everything be replaced? What about the sink and tub fixtures? What about the plumbing behind them? In short, if you're new to the field, how do you know what needs to be done?

The answer is that in this case, you need to get someone qualified out to see the entire property. Again, if you have a network or a dream team, it's easy. If you don't, it's a bit trickier, but certainly not impossible.

First, you must determine who you want to talk with. If it's a bathroom, a plumber certainly comes to mind. But, there are also people who do bathroom design, who work with plumbers, but who aren't plumbers themselves. There are people who refinish tubs and sinks without replacing them.

How do you learn about these alternatives? The only way is to talk to people in the trade, as many and as often as possible. And when you have a specific problem, ask people to come out to give you hard estimates.

Once again, if you're new, you'll have to let your fingers walk through the phone book to find people. Also, try the local newspaper where those who are more aggressively seeking work may advertise. Don't overlook signs on shops in the area.

Keep in mind, however, that if you don't already have a relationship with someone whom you want to get an estimate from—particularly a pro like a plumber or electrician—you're going to go on the bottom of their list. Chances are they're working during the day and will only be willing to come out at night . . . and then after they've already looked at the jobs who called in before you. Be prepared to wait (or make a contingent offer based on later inspections as noted in Chapter 6).

Logistics here can be tricky. You may need to schedule several people at different times over a couple of days. If the

*C*aution

_____

If you're going to get more than one estimate for the same job, try not to have those giving the estimate all be there at the same time. There's too much chance they'll compare notes and you'll only get a single figure answer!

house is vacant, that shouldn't be a problem. However, if an owner or, even worse, a tenant is there, it could be quite challenging.

My advice here is to be demanding and persistent. Remember, you're in the driver's seat when it comes to making an offer. A seller who wants to sell will have to do what it takes to get you to make that offer. If it means letting you and your estimators in five times during the day, then that's what it takes. Besides, usually with a fixer, the seller is aware that this is likely to happen and has preconditioned himself to accepting it.

When tenants are involved, however, it's a bit more problematic. The tenants have their privacy to lose and nothing to gain by letting you in a bunch of times. Again, be determined and persistent. If there's a problem, let the landlord/owner handle it. In a worst case, you may not be able to get in. But, if it's a terrific deal, you may want to make a guesstimate without an expert's estimate. If you do, however, leave a little extra in your offer for error.

One last problem may occur in getting an estimate from someone in the field and that may come about when you first call. One of the first questions they are likely to ask you is, "Do you own the property?"

These people intensely dislike going out and making estimates on deals that never get done. It's a waste of their valuable time. Hence, what they are really asking is whether or not you're a player. Are you the person who can hire them?

An owner certainly is. A buyer who has a deal in escrow certainly is. But, someone who's thinking about making an offer that may or may not get accepted is doubtful.

Of course, if you have a network and a dream team, it may be no problem. If you don't, you may need to tie up the property via a contingent offer (described in Chapter 6) before you're able to get people out. Or, you may just get lucky and find some really anxious tradespeople who want to bid on jobs and who want to get to know people like you.

Pricing Materials

You may need to install a new door, window, shower enclosure, kitchen sink, fireplace insert or almost anything else that you'll find in a house. You may need to know the cost of copper piping or a new circuit breaker box. How much are shingles that are approved for your area? (Today, some locales require special fireproof composition shingles; no wood is allowed. Some homeowners' associations only approve certain types and even brands.) Then there's the little stuff like nails, screws and tools themselves. What do all of these cost?

Assuming that you have a pretty good handle on what you want and need to do (as described above), your next stop may be a hardware store. In the past, hardware stores were the priciest of places to shop. If you weren't in the trade and able to buy wholesale, you often paid two or three times as much for hardware as those in the trade.

Today, however, with the various discount home maintenance franchises springing up all over the country, it's possible to purchase materials at quite reasonable cost, often for less than builders, as we'll see in a moment.

But first let's consider estimating materials costs. Most, but not all, materials that you'll need can be found at a discount hardware store. You may be able to get some things you need for less by shopping around, but a big discount hardware store often will give you a good average price. I suggest you simply go to one of the behemoths of the hardware field and price everything you need. Within a few hours you should have quite a detailed materials price list.

For unusual items, you'll need to shop around. For example, recently I needed to get the price on a septic sump pump. This is a special sludge pump that goes into a septic tank and pumps liquid waste uphill to a leech field. You'll usually only find it in rural areas without municipal sewer systems.

However, it is a specialty item not carried in any of the discount hardware stores I checked. In fact, it wasn't carried in any city within 50 miles of the property. However, I did locate an out-of-state plumbing supply house that not only had sump pumps, but over 35 different brands and models! They even put an engineer on the phone who, when I told him the height the pump would have to push the liquid and the size of the tank, gave me the precise size of pump I needed. And they were willing to ship it directly to me, if and when I ordered it using a credit card. As I said, you may need to shop around, but you will in every case (at least in every case in which I've been involved) ultimately be able to get a material's price, often over the phone.

Finding a Single Source

A few paragraphs ago, I mentioned that it was possible for you to not only get good prices, but also to get prices that were actually lower than what builders would pay. How can you do that? It works something like this.

Most people assume that when they need to buy something, virtually anything, they must pay top dollar, because they need to buy only one. You need a sink, so you go to the hardware store and buy one for close to full retail price. Even in a discount hardware store, you're paying more.

The reason is that we all assume that there are economies associated with buying in quantity. We've actually been conditioned into believing this from the time we were children. You go to the store and buy a pair of stockings and they are $5 apiece. But, if you buy three pair, you can get them for $12, or $4 apiece. The seller is willing to give you a discount because you buy in quantity. Sound familiar?

We all presume the same thing happens with building materials. We need to buy a shower enclosure. We go to a hardware store, even a discount hardware store, and buy one. We assume that whatever price we pay, it's got to be higher than a builder who goes directly to the manufacturer and buys 50 of these for a tract of houses he's building, right?

In reality, however, the truth is far different. When we need to purchase only one of an item, we may actually be at an advantage. We may be able to get a better price than that builder who purchases 50. The reason? We may be able to take advantage of closeouts, remainders and special sales.

No, this is not predictable and often you must act fairly quickly. But it does work. When you need to buy only one of an item, you can often get it for a fraction of its retail cost—if you look carefully.

Every hardware store, particularly the large discount ones, are trying to get rid of closeout items all the time. They often will mark them 50 percent off or more. Yes, sometimes they have a defect, but often it's only a scratch that you can hide or remove. Yes, it's hit-or-miss, and you can't predict what you'll find at any given time. But, if you're constantly on the lookout (as you will be, the more fixers you do), you'll buy generic items when they're available at closeout. And when you need something specific, you may check four or five stores before you find it at a price you want.

Thus, when pricing materials, if you're the sort who's willing to nose around in order to find the closeout, the remainder or the special sale, you may be able to take a percentage off the prices you see for the items sold at retail (even at discount) on store shelves. For myself, when it comes to big-ticket items such as sinks, doors, tubs, etc., I always figure a third less than I see them priced. Yes, it's a gamble. But I've had enough success at it that I just know that before I actually need the item (but after I've bought the property), I'll be able to find just one of it at a fraction of the cost I usually see posted.

Note that this also applies to labor. When a builder hires labor, he must deal with subcontractors, unions and pay scales. On the other hand, when you hire labor for your one job, you may be able to deal with an individual worker, often one who is doing the job on his own time.

As a result, you may be able to negotiate a better price. When you're asking a professional plumber or an electrician to bid on a job as part of his regular work, he's likely to give you a full-price bid. However, if he's doing it on his off hours to make a little extra money, he may be willing and able to do it for much less. After all, cutting his prices benefits both of you. It saves you money and gives him some extra work. This usually only works, however, when you have a small, single project to do. On the other hand, it's a great way to draw a professional in the trade into your dream team.

Do It Yourself or Hire It Out?

Finally, with regard to the guesstimate sheet, you'll notice that I include a column you can check for jobs that you intend doing yourself, as opposed to hiring labor out. It's important that you check here if you really do intend to do the work. The reason is that it could affect the pricing.

And this leads us to a subject that is one of the most contentious in the whole field of fixing up properties: the war between doing it yourself and hiring someone else to do it for you.

As every person who has worked on a fixer knows, if you do it yourself you should be able to save money. Depending on the job you may be able to do it quicker, better and cheaper than hiring someone else. At least, that's what we all want to believe. The truth, however, may be far different.

Always ask these three questions with regard to doing the work yourself versus paying others to do it:

1. Do you know how to do the work?

2. Do you have the time? (Or is your time better spent elsewhere?)

3. Does it really save you money?

You may think you know the answer to these questions and that the answer always is to DO IT YOURSELF! But, I would beg to differ. More often than we may realize, it turns out that it's quicker, easier, better and cheaper to have someone else do it for us. The example that quickly springs to mind is insulation.

Have you ever installed insulation? Most of us think that any fool can do it. You just unroll it (it usually comes in long tightly wound rolls) in the attic or, if it's an exposed wall, place it between the studs. What could be easier?

A whole lot could be easier. There's the matter of getting it where you want it. Pushing large rolls through a tiny attic access hole is not my idea of fun. Getting scratched all over by microscopic particles of rock wool or fiberglass is not my idea of fun, either. Finally, getting it to lay down evenly, everywhere is no easy feat.

I can recall I was once converting a garage to guest quarters. I was putting in a bathroom and bedroom over the garage. I needed to have insulation installed on the ceilings and walls, which were all exposed and easily accessible. So I went out and priced the insulation. I found out what it would cost me at the best discount. Then, more or less just for the heck of it, I called up someone who installed insulation professionally and had them come out to give me a bid. Their price, installed, was less than my cost to buy the material alone! Guess whether I did the work or hired it out?

Can You Do as Good a Job?

Of course, with insulation it really doesn't matter a whole lot whether the job is okay or really good. After all, once the wall covering is on, no one sees the work. The same applies to plumbing. Who cares if when you sweat a joint on copper piping it looks like Frankenstein's Monster's scar? All that matters is that it hold up to water pressure. Nobody's going to see what it looks like.

On the other hand, some jobs are *all* show. These include:

- Painting
- Plastering
- Wallpapering
- Wood finishing
- Carpet installation
- Tile installation

How well (or how poorly) you do here is obvious to anyone who looks. And if that person happens to be a potential buyer, and if the work looks terrible, you could lose your resale.

Does that mean that you should hire all of those jobs out, even painting? Not necessarily. There are certain jobs that you can learn quickly and do well enough to get by on the first or second attempt. These include painting as well as much plumbing and electrical work.

Many of these tasks you can learn how to do out of a book. And, in most cases you know immediately if you did a good job or not. Either it leaks or it doesn't. Either the paint looks great or it looks really bad.

On the other hand, some jobs require a lot of skill and training. For example, taping plasterboard. It's as simple as putting mud (wallboard paste) and taping across a joint. Any child of 10 can do it. However, to do it right so that the wall is smooth and the seam doesn't show takes practice and skill. I've done it maybe 50 times and I'm just getting to the point where I feel my work is coming close to looking professional.

If you aren't skilled at taping and texturing, it's well worth the money to get a pro to do it. It's not just the money here. It's a matter of getting a finished job that looks good.

Do You Have the Time?

I have yet to see a fixer project where there wasn't some sort of time constraint. Usually it's money. You only have so much money and that translates into so many months of mortgage payments before you must have the place finished and either move in or sell. It's been said over and over and it's still true: time is money.

Yes, you can do the plumbing work on the fixer. But, if *you* do it, it may take a month. If you hire an expert, it may take three days. Can you afford to waste the extra 27 days? What about the other work you could be doing if you weren't fooling around with the plumbing?

Don't ever overlook time or it will come back to haunt you. You only have so long to complete the work on every fixer you do. Be sure you factor in that time constraint when making the decision about who is going to do the work.

Are You Willing To Work for Free?

There's another point to consider. Your effort is worth something in terms of real money. If you don't believe that, then you could be in trouble.

Consider a friend of mine, Tim, who does his guesstimating along these lines. Tim looks mainly for cosmetic fixers. I've been along when he finds one and, since he thinks out loud, it's easy to follow his reasoning. It goes something like this:

"Painting all walls and ceilings. I guess I can do that."

"Putting in a new water heater. Yeah, I can do that."

"Installing a new furnace and air-conditioning. I've never done that, but what the heck, how hard can it be?

"Putting new stucco on the front and one side. It can't be that difficult to slap some cement on a wall. Okay, I'll do that."

"Roof leaks. I better put on a new roof as well. Oh what the heck, how long can it take to slap down some shingles. I'll do that, too."

You get the idea. Pretty soon, there's only one laborer on the job, Tim. And not to knock him, he's pretty good. But he's not a professional painter, plumber, plasterer or roofer. He's had some real disasters, fixers that he's done where he had to sell them again as fixers even after he'd done the work! Nobody would believe his work quality was acceptable—every buyer discounted those properties when he was trying to resell them.

Plus, it always takes Tim longer to do the job. He might spend nine months on a fixer, whereas I might spend three. During those nine months, however, he's paying mortgage interest, taxes, insurance and so on. Sometimes what he gains by doing the labor himself, albeit slower, he loses by paying out on holding costs.

The real problem with Tim, of course, is in his guesstimating. By never writing in a realistic figure for labor, he's always able to offer more for properties than others of us who add in labor costs. Tim does probably get more than his fair share of fixers this way. But, needless to say, Tim has lost more money than he'd care to admit on many of his jobs because he's attempted to do too much himself. It's important to not be a Tim when you work on a fixer.

What Is Your Work Actually Worth?

But, if your work *is* worth something, just what is that value? How do you place a price tag on it? The temptation is to say your work's not worth anything, because it's done in your spare or extra time. Yet, if you weren't working on a fixer, you could be working at some other salaried job. Or you could be relaxing in front of the TV with a glass of wine or a bottle of beer. Trading off those moments to relax has to be worth something, too.

So, how do you calculate how much your time is worth, say on an hourly basis? Here are three methods, any of which may work for you:

1. What could you make working for someone else at your regular job, if you weren't working on a fixer? If you're an hourly worker, then it's easy to judge. Just figure your hourly wage, whatever it might be. If, for example, you make $15 an hour, and the job on the fixer requires three hours of time to do, by your estimate, put down $45. That's what it's going to cost you to do it yourself.

    If you get a weekly or monthly salary, it's not hard to calculate your hourly wage. Just divide your salary by 40 hours a week or 160 hours a month, the standard work schedule.

2. What would a professional charge to do the work? Here you determine, as closely as possible, what it would cost a professional to do the work that's needed. For example, you need to install a water

heater. You could call a plumber. Or you could call a handyman.

My feeling is that you should figure what it would cost to call the cheapest pro to do the job. A plumber might charge you $60 a hour or more plus transportation time to and from your site. A handyman, on the other hand, might simply charge a flat fee, say $100, to install the water heater. If it took him four hours to do it, that's $25 an hour. In this case, I would figure the costs of labor if I were to do it at $25 an hour.

Keep in mind that in certain cases you may want to go with the higher figure. For example, let's say that instead of a water heater, you needed fittings sweated onto copper pipe to fix up a bathroom. Here, a handyman simply might not be up to the job. In this case, I would charge myself the plumber's fee.

3. Finally, what would you make if you took a part-time job to earn extra money, instead of working on the fixer? This is a bit trickier to do because part-time work that you do on the side usually doesn't pay the same as your regular work. Often it's done piecemeal and you may end up getting more or less an hour than for your regular job.

    A good way to judge is to think back to any side jobs you've recently had and use them as guides. If you haven't had any, consider what you might do as an alternative to fixing up the property. Then try to come as close to determining what your hourly wage would be. This is what you'll put down.

It doesn't matter which of the three methods you use. They are all arbitrary. The whole point, however, is to give yourself a wage for your work. By putting some reasonable figure down, you'll be getting a more realistic cost for fixing up the property.

In addition, should something go awry with your plans—if you get sick, you run out of time, the job's harder than you thought—you'll be able to afford to hire someone else to do the work without ruining your guesstimate. Further, should things go well, then when you ultimately resell, you will actually get paid what you are worth for the work you did!

For more information on this subject, I suggest you look into my book *The Home Remodeling Organizer* (Dearborn, 1995).

Can You Reduce Your Overhead Costs?

Finally, there's the matter of overhead costs. "What?" you may be saying, "I don't have any overhead." Actually, those costs may be there without your even knowing about it. To illustrate the point, consider this example of Jack, a person I hired a few years back to do some landscaping work on a fixer.

Jack was a big guy. He was making a living working with a partner as a handyman. He gave me a low bid of around $6,000 for doing some landscaping, cement work and fencing. I felt he and his partner were capable of doing the job and so I hired them.

Jack wanted some money up front, to buy about half the supplies and equipment needed to get started, and I gave him $2,000. He immediately bought a pager and a cellular phone. He also bought stationery, business cards and flyers to distribute through neighborhoods advertising his services.

When I reminded him that the money was supposed to go for the work on my fixer, he told me not to worry. He had it all under control. This was just some things he needed to do to expand his business. The next day he showed up with a new pick-up truck he had purchased, to help move supplies to the job.

The upshot of this true story is that within a week, Jack had spent the entire $2,000 I had given him on what might be termed overhead, items he felt were essential to doing his work, but which did not directly contribute to the job. Then he came back to me looking slackfaced and admitted he needed more money, to buy the supplies that the original money was to go for.

I refused to give him another dime. Instead, I went out and bought the needed supplies and had them delivered. Then I gave him a week to get the job done. During the week I bought the remainder of the supplies needed to complete the job.

Jack did the work with his partner and the job was done in an acceptable fashion. When they came in for their pay, I told them I owed them $4,000 more. However, the supplies had cost a total of $3,600. I handed them $400 in cash and got a receipt.

Jack and his partner walked out with $200 apiece looking as though they had been struck by lightning. I remember him saying, "Only $200 bucks, for all that work!" I reminded him that he had already received $2,000, but had blown it on overhead. He nodded and said, "Oh yeah, that stuff."

I'm not suggesting that you might be as foolish as Jack. However, once you get started on a job, you may find the temptation to spend your money on items not directly related to the work almost overpowering.

For example, you might find that you need a new drill. You can get a consumer unit at Sears that will do the job for $40, or, you can get a professional quality DeWalt or Milwaukee for probably twice that amount. The temptation to say that you'll use it time and again and it will pay for itself many times over will be strong. But, will that consumer unit suffice for all the work you do? Where will the money come from that you'll use to buy it? Will it come out of your labor costs or your materials costs?

Many savvy entrepreneurs who do fix-up work put in a figure for overhead. This includes money to spend on tools, on rental equipment, on a truck or on whatever else they'll need. Thus, when it comes time to buy tools to use on the job, they don't have any problem finding the funds for it.

The trouble, however, is that you're competing with others to get the house as cheaply as possible. Anything you add to your expenses reduces the price you can offer. Add 5 percent of the fix-up cost for overhead and you've reduced the price you'll offer for the property significantly. At the same time, a competitor may be figuring no overhead or only a 1 percent charge for it and that competition will come in with a bid much lower than yours.

My own feeling is that it's important to be as skimpy as possible with the tools for the job. This doesn't mean always buying the consumer model drill over the professional model. If it's something you're going to use over and over, the pro model may indeed be the best for you.

Similarly, you may indeed need a pick-up truck to haul supplies around, particularly if you're going to be doing fixers on a regular basis. But, do you need a new truck or will an old, beat-up but good running model do just as well? (Again, don't be pennywise and pound foolish. Sometimes you can buy on credit or lease a new vehicle for only a few hundred a month, compared to putting out capital to buy an old one for cash. Always compare costs to see what works best for you.)

Being skimpy means not spending any more money than absolutely necessary on overhead. You may need a diamond blade tile cutter to do tile work in the kitchen and bath. You can buy one for $500, or you can rent almost the same model for $25. Unless you're planning to go into the business of laying tile, rent it.

When you need business cards and stationery, you can go to a printer and pay $150 for the finest quality, or you can order out of a magazine and get acceptable quality for $20. Since your business is fixing up properties and not writing tomes, which should you get?

Don't let overhead bog you down. You need to spend something on tools and equipment. Just be sure it's as little as possible.

Bottom-Lining It

What it all comes down to is that when you decide to tackle a fixer, you enter a highly competitive field. And, as in any competitive arena, the profits go to the person who has the best calculations.

You need to know as accurately as possible what your labor costs are going to be whether you do the work or you hire it out. You need to know what your cost of materials is going to be. And you need to know pretty darn accurately how much you're going to need to spend, realistically, on overhead.

You can't do a fixer unless your offer is the one that's accepted by the seller. And if a competitor offers just $500 more than you do for the same property (and has roughly the same deal and creditworthiness), whose offer do you think the seller will accept? Just remember, $500 may only be the cost of one piece of equipment, one bathtub, or hiring a pro to do a simple job.

In fixing up properties, the deals often go to the best guesstimator.

For additional information on this subject, check into my book *The Home Remodeling Organizer* (Dearborn, 1995).

FIGURE 11.1 Guesstimator's Sheet

Task	Hours	Labor		Materials	Overhead
		You	Hire It?		
KITCHEN					
Cabinet Cleaning					
Cabinet Painting					
Cabinet Refinish					
Cabinet Repair					
Cabinet Replace					
Ceiling Paint					
Ceiling Repair					
Counter Clean					
Counter Formica Install					
Counter Granite Install					
Counter Other Install					
Counter Repair					
Counter Tile Install					
Counter Wood Edge Install					
Dishwasher Fix					
Dishwasher Replace					
Electrical Fix					
Electrical Replace					
Faucets Replace					

FIGURE 11.1 Guesstimator's Sheet *(Continued)*

Task	Hours	Labor		Materials	Overhead
		You	Hire It?		
Faucets Washer Replace					
Floor Cleaning					
Floor Linoleum Install					
Floor Tile Install					
Floor Wood Install					
Garbage Disposal Fix					
Garbage Disposal Replace					
Plumbing Fix					
Sink Cleaning					
Sink Repair					
Sink Replace					
Smoke Alarm Install					
Stove Fix					
Stove Hood Fix					
Stove Hood Replace					
Stove Replace					
Wall Paint					
Wall Repair					
Window Cleaning					
Window Repair					

FIGURE 11.1 Guesstimator's Sheet *(Continued)*

Task	Hours	Labor		Materials	Overhead
		You	Hire It?		
Other					
Other					
Other					
BATHROOM					
Cabinet Cleaning					
Cabinet Painting					
Cabinet Refinish					
Cabinet Repair					
Cabinet Replace					
Ceiling Paint					
Ceiling Repair					
Counter Clean					
Counter Formica Install					
Counter Granite Install					
Counter Other Install					
Counter Repair					
Counter Tile Install					
Counter Wood Edge Install					
Electrical Fix					
Electrical Replace					
Faucets Replace					

FIGURE 11.1 Guesstimator's Sheet *(Continued)*

Task	Hours	Labor		Materials	Overhead
		You	Hire It?		
Faucets Washer Replace					
Floor Cleaning					
Floor Linoleum Install					
Floor Tile Install					
Floor Wood Install					
Sink Cleaning					
Sink Repair					
Sink Replace					
Smoke Alarm Install					
Toilet Cleaning					
Toilet Replace					
Towel Holders Replace					
Tub/Shower Clean					
Tub/Shower Curtain					
Tub/Shower Door					
Tub/Shower Drain Clean					
Tub/Shower Drain Fix					
Tub/Shower Refinish					
Tub/Shower Replace					
Wall Paint					

FIGURE 11.1 Guesstimator's Sheet *(Continued)*

Task	Hours	Labor		Materials	Overhead
		You	Hire It?		
Wall Repair					
Window Cleaning					
Window Repair					
Wood Rot Fix					
Other					
Other					
Other					
BEDROOM #					
Cabinet Cleaning					
Cabinet Painting					
Cabinet Refinish					
Cabinet Repair					
Cabinet Replace					
Carpet Clean					
Carpet Replace					
Ceiling Paint					
Ceiling Repair					
Closet Door Repair					
Closet Door Replace					
Closet Paint					
Counter Clean					

FIGURE 11.1 Guesstimator's Sheet *(Continued)*

Task	Hours	Labor		Materials	Overhead
		You	Hire It?		
Counter Repair					
Electrical Fix					
Electrical Replace					
Floor Cleaning					
Floor Wood Install					
Smoke Alarm Install					
Wall Paint					
Wall Repair					
Window Cleaning					
Window Repair					
Other					
Other					
Other					
LIVING ROOM					
Carpet Clean					
Carpet Replace					
Ceiling Paint					
Ceiling Repair					
Closet Door Repair					
Closet Door Replace					
Closet Paint					

FIGURE 11.1 Guesstimator's Sheet *(Continued)*

Task	Hours	Labor		Materials	Overhead
		You	Hire It?		
Electrical Fix					
Electrical Replace					
Fireplace Clean					
Fireplace Fix					
Fireplace Replace					
Floor Cleaning					
Floor Wood Install					
Smoke Alarm Install					
Stairway Fix					
Wall Paint					
Wall Repair					
Window Cleaning					
Window Repair					
Other					
Other					
Other					
DINING ROOM					
Carpet Clean					
Carpet Replace					
Ceiling Paint					
Ceiling Repair					

FIGURE 11.1 Guesstimator's Sheet *(Continued)*

Task	Hours	Labor		Materials	Overhead
		You	Hire It?		
Closet Door Repair					
Closet Door Replace					
Closet Paint					
Electrical Fix					
Electrical Replace					
Fireplace Clean					
Fireplace Fix					
Fireplace Replace					
Floor Cleaning					
Floor Wood Install					
Smoke Alarm Install					
Stairway Fix					
Wall Paint					
Wall Repair					
Window Cleaning					
Window Repair					
Other					
Other					
Other					
FAMILY ROOM					
Carpet Clean					

FIGURE 11.1 Guesstimator's Sheet *(Continued)*

Task	Hours	Labor You	Labor Hire It?	Materials	Overhead
Carpet Replace					
Ceiling Paint					
Ceiling Repair					
Closet Door Repair					
Closet Door Replace					
Closet Paint					
Electrical Fix					
Electrical Replace					
Fireplace Clean					
Fireplace Fix					
Fireplace Replace					
Floor Cleaning					
Floor Wood Install					
Stairway Fix					
Wall Paint					
Wall Repair					
Window Cleaning					
Window Repair					
Other					
Other					
Other					

FIGURE 11.1 Guesstimator's Sheet *(Continued)*

Task	Hours	Labor		Materials	Overhead
		You	Hire It?		
Other					
ENTRANCE/HALLWAY					
Carpet Clean					
Carpet Replace					
Ceiling Paint					
Ceiling Repair					
Closet Door Repair					
Closet Door Replace					
Closet Paint					
Electrical Fix					
Electrical Replace					
Floor Cleaning					
Floor Wood Install					
Stairway Fix					
Wall Paint					
Wall Repair					
Window Cleaning					
Window Repair					
Other					
Other					
Other					

FIGURE 11.1 Guesstimator's Sheet *(Continued)*

Task	Hours	Labor		Materials	Overhead
		You	Hire It?		
ATTIC					
Electrical Fix					
Electrical Replace					
Fans Fix					
Fans Install					
Insulation Add					
Insulation Install					
Plumbing Fix					
Plumbing Replace					
Other					
Other					
Other					
BASEMENT/GARAGE					
Electrical Fix					
Electrical Replace					
Floor Cracks Fix					
Floor Replace					
Furnace/Air Fix					
Furnace/Air Replace					
Lights Fix					
Lights/Install					

FIGURE 11.1 Guesstimator's Sheet *(Continued)*

Task	Hours	Labor		Materials	Overhead
		You	Hire It?		
Plumbing Fix					
Plumbing Replace					
Stairs Fix					
Stairs Replace					
Water Heater Fix					
Water Heater Replace					
Other					
Other					
Other					
EXTERIOR					
Chimney Install					
Chimney Repair					
Chimney Replace					
Drainage Fix					
Driveway Clean					
Driveway Fix					
Driveway Replace					
Entrance Clean					
Entrance Paint					
Fence Install					
Fence Paint					

FIGURE 11.1 Guesstimator's Sheet *(Continued)*

Task	Hours	Labor		Materials	Overhead
		You	Hire It?		
Fence Repair					
Front Door Clean					
Front Door Install					
Front Door Paint					
Gutters Clean					
Gutters Fix					
Gutters Install					
Lawn Plant					
Lawn Reseed					
Patio Fix					
Patio Install					
Pool Clean					
Pool Fix					
Roof Repair					
Roof Replace					
Screens Replace					
Shrubs Plant					
Shrubs Trim					
Spa Clean					
Spa Fix					
Walks Clean					

FIGURE 11.1 Guesstimator's Sheet *(Continued)*

Task	Hours	Labor		Materials	Overhead
		You	Hire It?		
Walks Fix					
Walks Replace					
Walls Paint					
Walls Patch					
Windows Clean					
Windows Replace					
Other					
Other					
Other					

CHAPTER 12

Quick Cosmetic Fixes

The most popular type of fixer is undoubtedly the "cosmetic" fixer. As explained in Chapter 2, there's basically nothing wrong with a cosmetic fixer's structure. It just looks bad. The paint throughout may be old, stained, dirty or even peeling. There may be cracked windows. Sinks may be broken or missing. The carpet may be stained, torn or worn out. The yard usually is totally run down, the lawn and shrubbery dead or dying. Typically the cosmetic fixer is the worst-looking fixer you can find.

As we've seen, however, there's little seriously wrong with such a property. Appearances are the main problem. Fixing up, therefore, is mainly a matter of cleaning, repairing or replacing nonstructural items, and painting.

This doesn't mean, however, that dealing with a cosmetic fixer is inexpensive or simple. You can lose money here just as fast as with a "scraper," if you don't know what you're doing. In this chapter, we're going to look at some tricks I've discovered over the years when dealing with the cosmetic fixer. I hope you will profit from these tricks.

How Much Do You Need To Clean Up?

As noted, the typical cosmetic fixer is a mess. Very often, the previous owners either had rented the property out to tenants who almost destroyed it, or the owners went into foreclosure and took their anger and frustration out on the house. Thus, your first task is going to be to clean up. Indeed, it's very important to remember that you may not be able to see the total amount of repair work you need to do until the property is cleaned up.

My suggestion is that you hire someone else to do the basic clean up. People are available who do this professionally and they are very inexpensive to hire. For example, I recently had a home I purchased to fix up and it had a very large yard, both behind and in front. The trees were overgrown, all kinds of trash had been dumped in the back yard (including the remains of an old Plymouth Barracuda automobile!) and the front yard had weeds as tall as my waist. I could have rented a truck and spent a week (and a lot of backaches) getting rid of all of this stuff. Instead, I hired a crew who I found from their ad in the local paper. They had their own large truck and for $300, they trimmed, mowed and cleaned everything up. And they did it all in one day!

The same applies to the inside. For around $100, you should be able to hire a cleaning crew to come in and clean up bathrooms, kitchen, windows and walls. They will probably take less than half a day and do a better job than you could do in three or four days.

Cleaning Carpets

A special word, however, needs to be said about the limitations of clean up with regard to walls, ceilings and carpets—carpets first. You probably won't really know the condition of the carpeting until you've had the house cleaned up and the carpet at least thoroughly vacuumed. Once that's done, you need to decide whether you want a thorough carpet cleaning or you want to just replace what's there. Check for the following:

Are there dark-colored stains in areas that are likely to be out in the open (have no furniture)? For example, if you have a beige carpet in the living room and there's a red stain from some berry juice (something almost impossible to get out), you're going to need to forget about cleaning and think about recarpeting at least that room.

On the other hand, if the carpet in the living room is okay, but there's some grease stains on the carpet by the sliding glass door leading to the patio, you may want to have a thorough carpet cleaning done. Grease stains look bad, but with the powerful degreasers available today, they often will come completely out.

Ask someone who knows about cleaning carpet to tell you which stains will come out and which won't. Carpet cleaners will often come to your property to give you a bid. (Avoid those who offer to clean for ridiculously low fees such as $7 a room. You won't get more than what you pay for.) When a cleaning person says he won't guarantee a stain will come out, it usually means it won't come out. Save your money and don't clean—replace.

In addition to stains, check the nap of the carpet. Look particularly in heavy traffic areas such as entrances to rooms and hallways. If the carpet is worn to the point where it's laying down and looks matted, again you're probably better off saving your money and not cleaning it—just replace it. Cleaning will make a dirty carpet look better, but it won't make an old carpet look new. Besides, the cost of recarpeting may be far less than you imagine, as we'll find out shortly.

Cleaning Walls

Cleaning walls is a no-no, except in kitchens and baths where a high-gloss paint is used. In living rooms, dining rooms, bedrooms, etc., stains on walls often cannot be easily cleaned off, particularly if the wall hasn't been recently painted. What happens is that the entire wall area gets dirty over time. When you scrub to remove a small stain, you actually clean an area of the wall making it look lighter than the remainder of the wall. Now you must clean more of the wall to make things look even. Soon, you're trying to clean the entire wall. While the results here are dubious, keep in mind that it only takes a short while to repaint a wall, usually much less time and effort than is required to clean it.

On the other hand, I've had good success with spot repainting of walls, as long as (1) the area to be touched up is fairly tiny and (2) it's been less than a year since the wall was completely painted. (Any longer than a year and you run into a problem similar to that of cleaning dirt described above.)

Cleaning Tile

Tile will normally clean up very well with a strong cleaning agent. Grout between tiles, however, can be a different story. If it's white or light-colored and old (or very new), it will often absorb dirt and turn a mottled shade of brown.

Using a common toothbrush with cleanser can have a good effect here, but plan to spend a long time at it. An alternative would be to regrout, particularly easy to do if the current grout is old and a surface layer ($1/16$" or more) can be quickly removed to leave room for new grout. (Forget it if you have to remove all of the grout—it's so much work you're better off retiling.)

Cleaning Bathrooms

A big problem here is not so much dirt as calcium deposits and mildews. Fortunately, very efficient mildew and calcium removers are available. You can often clean up here in a few minutes with these liquids. Only keep the windows open and use a fan to get good air circulation—they're strong!

A word of warning: Don't spill the above strong cleaners or any bleach you may use to clean bathrooms on carpeting. They won't stain the carpeting so much as bleach the color out. With modern synthetic carpets, this can mean you'll end up with unsightly "dots" of bright color such as yellow, which may be the carpet's uncolored look.

Front Doors

Don't bother to clean. Slap a new coat of paint on. It will be easier, take less time and look a whole lot better.

If the paint isn't too bad in the entranceway, try using a hose with a high-pressure nozzle. You can quickly remove a lot of spider webs and dirt this way.

Ceilings

If the ceiling is simply painted, then reread the paragraphs above on cleaning walls. However, many houses have acoustical material blown onto the ceiling. Over time this gets dirty and discolored. The worst part is that this process often happens unevenly.

If you have a dirty acoustical ceiling, you really only have two choices. You can paint it or have it reblown. Reblowing can cost around $1 a square foot. Because of the expense, many people involved with fixers choose to repaint. This is probably a mistake because when painting over an acoustical ceiling, the underlying material often absorbs huge amounts of paint. By the time you buy dozens of gallons of paint, put it on and redo it several times to get it right, you would probably be better off reblowing. Contact a contractor who specializes in this work.

What Should You Paint?

We've already noted some areas that should be painted and not cleaned. But there are other areas where painting is almost mandatory.

The entrance, living room, dining room, kitchen and baths and the master bedroom should be painted (after the walls are patched). The reason is that new paint looks fresh and good. It's like new clothes—appealing. It will make buyers want to purchase the property.

The same holds true for the front of the house and any other side that faces the street. First impressions are critical when reselling and nothing makes a worse first impression than dirty walls or peeling paint.

You can sometimes get by with not painting hallways and other bedrooms, if they're not too badly beaten up. You can almost always get by with not painting closets or the inside of drawers and cabinets.

Be sure you do put a nice new coat of high-gloss paint on kitchens and bathrooms, unless the existing paint is in good shape and any marks can be quickly and easily removed.

Should You Put In New Carpeting?

Unless the property has quality hardwood, tile, granite or other expensive-looking floors, recarpet (unless you can clean existing good-quality carpet, as noted above). Most people think of recarpeting, particularly an entire house, as incredibly expensive. It isn't cheap, but it's nowhere near as expensive as you may imagine.

First, remember that when it's new, even a lower grade of modern carpeting looks terrific and will continue to look terrific for at least a year or two.

Second, installing new carpeting is much cheaper today than it was ten years ago because of the new type of threads that are used (which are frequently resistant to stain and matting), as well as the many new mills that produce carpeting.

Third, in almost every major city, there are carpet wholesalers that deal direct with the public. If you go to a carpet showroom or a department store to buy carpeting, you'll pay top dollar. But, if you buy from a wholesaler, you can often get excellent carpeting at deep discounts. Today, minimally acceptable carpeting can be installed for $10 a yard, quite good carpeting for $15 and excellent looking carpeting for $20. This isn't to say that you can't pay more. You can. The sky's the limit with quality carpeting. But, for a cosmetic fixer, it's hardly worth it.

Should You Install New Counters and Fixtures?

In a cosmetic fixer, often the existing countertops and fixtures such as sinks, tubs and toilets have been damaged. If so, then you must replace them. Of course, the question remains of the quality to use. My suggestion is to make the quality match the neighborhood. If you're in a $600,000 neighborhood, don't scrimp on the fixtures and countertops. On the other hand, if you're planning on selling the house for $125,000, formica and stainless steel will do very well, thank you!

The real decisions come about when the old fixtures are merely dirty or scratched, but not broken. Should you clean and fix or replace?

Old porcelain tubs and sinks can be refinished and if the work is done well, they look as good as new. However, the cost of refinishing is often much more than the cost of materials to replace. Of course, there's also the cost of labor.

My suggestion is that you use two criteria to help you judge whether to fix or replace fixtures. First, is it difficult to get to the fixture so that a lot of labor cost will be involved? If so, seriously consider refinishing.

Second, is the fixture old-fashioned and out-of-date? If it is, consider replacing it, even if it's in good shape. Old-fashioned fixtures are a turn-off to buyers, all of whom pay special attention to kitchens and bathrooms.

By the way, don't confuse old-fashioned with classic. Many brand-new sinks, tubs and showers look like turn-of-the-century models, when actually they are high-fashion.

Unless the faucets are near new, they should be replaced. A good-looking chrome faucet assembly can be purchased for $50 or less and installed in less than an hour. It's well worth the money for the sharp look it gives.

Light fixtures fit in the same category. You want lots of light, particularly in dark corners where sunlight doesn't easily reach. New light fixtures are very inexpensive. (You can, of course, pay a fortune for some, but unless you've got the $600,000 house, the higher-priced models aren't really needed.)

Get fixtures that put out a lot of light and look good. They help dress up a property and make it much more saleable.

In terms of countertops, the decision is tougher. It costs a lot of money to put in a nice new tile counter. Use granite or other exotic material and the price goes through the roof. Yet, as noted earlier, if the neighborhood warrants it, spend the bucks. It will dramatically increase your chances of a sale.

On the other hand, in more modest areas, tile or even formica, as noted earlier, will do. Or, if the existing counter-tops do not look bad, a grout and surface cleaning may be all that's needed.

Should Roofs Be Fixed or Replaced?

Roofs are a big-ticket expense. A good new roof on an average-sized house can cost anywhere from $3,000 to $25,000 or more. It all depends on the type of material that you use. (Often CC&Rs—conditions, covenants and restrictions—or homeowners' associations will dictate the minimum quality roof that can be installed.)

Hence, there's a real incentive to make do with the roof that you've got. Why not save a bundle and fix instead of replace?

It all depends on two factors: Does the roof leak and does it look good?

Most wood roofs will continue to look okay, even after they reach the point where they leak like sieves. On the other hand, an inexpensive composition shingle roof can look terrible, yet hold out water just fine.

My own feeling is that the roof must look good in order to resell the property. Usually the single biggest part of the property that buyers see when they drive up is the roof. If the shingles are discolored and curled, it diminishes the entire property's value. Therefore, my suggestion is that if the roof looks bad, fix it regardless of whether it leaks or not. But, use the least expensive roofing material possible that fits in with the quality of the neighborhood. (Some high-end neighborhoods only have tile roofs, for example. That's what you'll have to use. However, if every other house on the block has a composition shingle roof, why put anything better on yours?)

Hint

Today there are shingles composed of fiberglass and other materials that are quite inexpensive, yet have a high-quality, three-dimensional appearance and also have a high fire resistance rating. I recently did a roof on a house and a detached garage made of these materials and the entire price was only $3,300 including labor! It's something to check out.

Leaking is another matter. Most wood roofs leak. That's why tar paper or similar material is often laid underneath—to keep the water out. What this means is that as long as the tar paper is intact, you can cosmetically fix the wood roof by inserting new shingles where the old ones have fallen out. It's not a big chore and it ends up looking good. Only, if you do it yourself, be careful you don't fall off the roof!

Fixing the tar paper, on the other hand, is a different story. If there are only a couple of rips and tears here and there, it probably can be done fairly easily. However, if the sun has gotten to the paper and decomposed it, then it's a hopeless task. You could be patching forever and it would still leak. Bad paper underneath means a new roof job on top.

Tile roofs, once properly installed, never leak until the tile breaks. After that, stopping the leaking can be very difficult because tile roofs also use tar paper or something similar underneath to keep the water out. But, when tiles crack, their sharp edges will often perforate the tar paper beneath. You have to fix the tar paper before you can fix the tiles. But, if you try walking on, lifting or moving old tiles, chances are you'll only crack more of them.

If you have a tile roof that leaks, get an expert roofer out. Someone who really knows what he's doing may be able to patch it effectively. Otherwise, you could be up for a very expensive roof job.

Should You Paint or Replace Old Stucco?

Probably more than half the houses in America have stucco exteriors. It's essentially cement affixed to chicken wire and it looks good and lasts a long time.

Eventually, however, with sunlight constantly hitting it, a stucco wall will begin to look bad. It's at that point that you need to do something.

But experts will quickly point out that paint is actually inside the final coat of stucco. That means, they say, that you should only restucco (with new paint in the mixture), not paint. Is that true?

Technically, it is. If you want a long-lasting job, restucco, don't repaint. However, if you want a job that will look good for five or ten years, paint. I always do. Restuccoing will cost thousands of dollars. I can usually get an exterior, as long as it's not too big, repainted in the hundreds. And by the way, use a latex paint. It lasts better than oil paint on stucco and is far easier to clean up.

Should You Scrape Wood Clean and Trim Before Paint?

The rule book says always scrape before repainting. The reason is obvious. If you paint over loose existing chips of paint, it will all eventually give way and flake off.

However, the truth is somewhat different. The reason paint flakes and chips off is often twofold. First, moisture got under the original coat of paint as it was drying and prevented it from adhering properly. A second possible cause was that the original paint was cheap, hence it deteriorated rapidly from weathering.

My suggestion is that if you don't need a highly polished finished look, but can instead use a rustic look, that you use a metal scraper to get off the very loose, chipping material. But don't fight to remove the paint that's sticking well. If it's sticking now, it'll be sticking ten years from now, as long as moisture doesn't lift it off.

Use a thick paint (some say oil is better), and cover the wood and the old strongly adhering paint. Use a seal first, if possible. Be sure to paint the edges of the wood and not just the flat surfaces. Water gets in from the edges.

The reason, of course, is that it takes ten times the effort to remove old paint as it does to put new paint on. Yes, it's okay to paint over the old. Just be careful to remove any loose existing paint.

Should You Plant from Seed or Put In Sod Lawn?

The answer here should be fairly straightforward. For a 1,000-square-foot lawn, it costs about $15 to plant from seed and about a thousand dollars to put in sod. $15 versus $1,000? Now, which should I do?

Of course, there is some exaggeration here. You do need to use more fertilizer with seed. But the ground needs to be prepared for both types of lawn, with actually more preparation for sod.

The difference is in the results. If you use a good quality of fresh sod, you'll have a fabulous, thick lawn in a matter of days. If you use a good-quality seed with proper ground preparation and adequate fertilizer, it will take several months to achieve a lawn that looks even remotely close to sod.

However, if you're fixing up a property, you probably do have several months. That's why I suggest that you plant the lawn as your first order of business. That way, while you're patching, fixing and painting, you can be watering the lawn and watching it grow. A few months later, when your main work is done, the lawn is ready.

No, it probably still won't look as good as sod. That could take a lot of care and many months. But it can look adequate. And that, of course, is all that counts in a cosmetic fixer.

The same holds true with shrubs and bushes. If you have the time, buy them young and small and let them grow. Only if you don't have time, should you spend the extra bucks to buy them fully grown.

What about Air-Conditioning, a New Heater or New Plumbing?

These are big-ticket items and you normally don't need to worry about them in a cosmetic fixer. I wouldn't even bother to put in a new water heater, unless the old one leaks.

Remember, with a cosmetic fixer, what you want to do is to fix those things that look bad. Appearance is everything. In the next chapter, we'll deal with the big items that are very costly to fix or replace, but which you can't easily see.

CHAPTER 13

Working Around the Big Problem

Occasionally you'll run into a fixer that has a single big problem. It could be a rejuvenator or a broken-back fixer. What counts is that there is something so wrong with the property that it drives the value down and thus makes it a good candidate for your efforts.

What could such a problem be? I can recall one fixer that was over 80 years old and was heated exclusively by fireplaces. It simply had no modern heating system of any kind. What was worse, it had a tiny crawlspace instead of a basement, so installing a furnace below was impossible. The solution was to install a forced-air furnace and central air conditioner in the attic with attic and wall ducts. The solution was relatively inexpensive.

Working around the big problem in this kind of fixer involves at least three elements: recognition of the true problem, creativity in finding a solution and execution in fixing it properly. We'll cover each as a separate heading.

How To Recognize the Problem

You'd think that the easiest part of dealing with a "big-problem" fixer is recognizing it. But, I've found that very often that's simply not the case. Many times, the hardest part is determining exactly what the problem really is.

For example, not long ago I was looking at an expensive property in the $300,000 range. What enticed me was that the owner was asking $50,000 less than I'd expect the property to sell for.

Now a $50,000 cut in price usually means something is significantly wrong. However, the two-story house was only about 11 years old, seemed to be in fairly good shape (cosmetically speaking) and was well located in a good neighborhood. It seemed too good a deal to be true . . . and it was.

When I asked the seller why he had reduced the price, I was told, "The house has a 'cracked slab' and we want a quick sale. We're selling it strictly 'as is.'"

"Cracked Slabs"

The seller used two terms there that immediately put me on guard: "cracked slab" and "as is."

Houses in many parts of the country are built on top of a slab of concrete. Typically there is a peripheral foundation that goes down 18 inches or 2 feet, but the slab itself is poured over sand and a membrane (used to keep moisture out) and is typically only 4 to 6 inches thick. When it cracks, the house on top of it can shift, leading to cracks in walls and ceilings.

The thing about slabs, however, is that they almost all crack. That's why they have reinforcing steel inside them. Even if the cement is broken, the steel holds the pieces together. Once the causative problem for the cracking (often bad water runoff) is corrected, the slab stabilizes for the life of the property. I've owned many properties with apparently severe slab cracking, and it hasn't been a problem. Therefore, I was not overly concerned about the cracked slab, although I certainly wanted to scrutinize it more.

"As Is" Sales

What was of greater concern to me was the owner's insistence that the sale be "as is," that the owner would not warrant the property no matter what was wrong.

It's important to understand that in today's marketplace, there really is no such thing as an "as is" sale, at least not in terms of what it used to mean. In years gone by, selling "as is" meant the buyer bought blind. The seller didn't disclose anything about the property and the purchaser agreed not to come back at the seller with complaints after the sale, no matter what was wrong. The buyer truly was purchasing a "pig in a poke."

Today, in almost all parts of the country, sellers must disclose all problems no matter if they write in "as is." Further, buyers are entitled to an inspection. Then, if problems are found, negotiations typically follow, which result in a lower price because of the problem. Buyers aren't able to complain to the seller after the sale, when everything is disclosed, and in that sense property sales are "as is." But in the bigger scheme of things, since everything is presumably out in the open, buyers really aren't buying a pig in a poke, and the old meaning of "as is" is gone.

Thus, only a foolish seller attempts today to sell "as is" because those two words alert buyers that there's a serious problem with a property, nor do they grant the seller much protection at all.

Thus, when this seller told me he was selling "as is," my "be careful" antenna went up. Maybe he was simply a seller who didn't realize how selling this way sounded. Or maybe

Hint

If you're a seller, it's usually best to simply disclose problems and warrant the property in the usual way. Attempting to sell "as is" only makes buyers wary and gives you less protection than you may think.

he was really foolish and was trying to conceal something. Whichever way it came down, I figured it had something to do with the cracked slab, since that was the only potentially serious defect he had disclosed.

So I made my own inspection of the property. The seller was eager to point out some relatively minor cracks in the ceilings and walls of the second floor, which he said were due to the slab cracking. Nothing really unusual there, mostly cosmetic.

As we walked through the bottom floor, I asked him where the slab was cracked. He indicated there were a few cracks here and there, but they were under the wall-to-wall carpeting and couldn't be readily seen. If I made an offer on the property, of course, he would have the carpeting rolled back so I could look at them. Again, nothing unusual there.

Finally, we walked into the family room, which was by the garage on one side of the property. He pointed out a bigger-than-expected crack in the wall and ceiling, and said that the slab had a separation between the family room and the rest of the house. Although the visual cracks seemed severe, again I judged that they could be cosmetically covered, as long as they didn't get worse.

Then, as I was walked out of the family room into the garage, I noticed something odd. I kept tripping over my feet, as though they weren't working properly. I paused and looked back at the family room . . . and then it struck me. The room was not level. Although it was actually quite hard to see, the room had shifted so that it slanted downward on one side, as much as several inches I guessed. Now this was something more than just a cracked slab.

I went back in and took a large marble out of my pocket, which I carry for just such occasions. I placed it on the floor on one side of the room. It immediately rolled to the other side, over the carpeting. That indicated a serious slope.

When I asked the seller about the problem, he said it was simply the ground "settling."

Yes, ground does tend to settle under a house after it's built. However, the settling doesn't usually all take place in one direction. This was something else.

We moved outside and I scanned the lot. It had a high slope upward in the back, the house itself was on a level site and the ground sloped downward in front. Other houses on the street were similarly situated. But, there was something odd about the overall slope of the land.

When I moved to one side and tried to imagine the slope as it had been before the house was built, I immediately saw the problem. A notch had been cut out of the hillside to create the building site. However, the notch wasn't big enough to hold the whole house. So what probably had happened was that the dirt taken from the notch was dumped on the downside of the slope, thereby extending the building site out. Most of the house was built where the hillside had been notched. But the family room and garage had been built on the land that had been filled.

"Cutting and filling," as this technique is called, can work well, as long as the filled ground has been properly tamped down. This involves using special tampers or grading with heavy equipment to take all the "give" out of the soil. I guessed this had not been done.

As a result, the filled area was sinking, while the notched area remained firm. In short, the house was slowly splitting in half. The cracked slab was not the problem, but the symptom. And the remedy would have to be nothing less than lifting up the portion of the house that was falling, recompress the ground and then putting the house back.

Naturally the seller was offering a discount of $50,000. In my head I calculated that it would cost three or four times that amount to fix the problem, if indeed it could ever be fixed.

When I confronted the seller with my analysis, he didn't deny it, making me suspect he had known about it all along. He said that was why he had knocked $50,000 off the price. When I suggested the problem was far more serious than $50,000 could solve, he shrugged. That was all he was willing to discount.

In other words, he was waiting to hook some poor fish who would think that the cracked slab was the problem and who would buy thinking that a few cosmetic fixes would do the job. By the time the unwary buyer found out what the real trouble was, I suspected the seller would be long gone.

All of which is to say that discovering the true problem can be the biggest part of the battle. On the next page are some guidelines for you to follow when you're looking at a house that you suspect has a big problem.

Can You Find a Creative Solution?

Assuming you've discovered what the problem with the house is, your next task will be to come up with a solution. However, the more creative your solution, chances are the more money there is to be made on the deal for you because creative solutions often save money, big money. In our previous example of the cut-and-fill house, there was no creative

---

$\mathcal{G}$uidelines for Finding the Big Problem

1. Never rely entirely on what the seller says. Sellers may disclose only part of a problem.

2. Separate symptoms from cause. What you see may only be a symptom of a bigger problem that is not as easily visible.

3. Beware whenever a seller offers a property "as is." It may mean that there's a bigger hidden problem that you're overlooking.

4. Always inspect the property thoroughly yourself and don't jump to conclusions as you go through. Let your senses and your common sense guide you.

5. If you don't know or aren't sure, bring in an expert. Soil engineers are a good bet for houses that seem to have minor cracks.

---

solution to save money that I could find. It was simply going to cost a fortune to fix the place doing it the old-fashioned way. However, if there had been a creative solution, perhaps I could have bought the property for the seller's asking price and still made money. Consider this true example.

Rita was an entrepreneur who was very clever with fixers. She had done several and had always managed to make a good profit. Now she was looking at a home built on a hillside near west Los Angeles. As those familiar with the area know, property values there have risen so high that even marginal lots are used for home construction. Sometimes homes seem to jut right out of the hillsides on impossible slopes. They are often subject to the perils of erosion, earthquake and hillside fires.

This particular house had an erosion problem. It was built in a wash on a moderately steep lot. The house was on two levels going down the hillside.

Over time, however, the lot had slowly eroded. With each winter's rainfall, less of the lower end of the lot was left, until, when Rita saw it, the lower portion of the house was hanging out over space where land that had originally supported it had fallen away. The house was not on a slab, but instead had a wood frame and wood floor, and the foundation beams were hanging together just by the nails in them.

Of course, the house had been condemned by the building department and the owners had moved out. They had stopped making payments on their mortgage and the bank had foreclosed. Now the bank was trying to sell, but having a hard time of it.

Rita discovered that the bank wanted to sell for land value only, figuring the house was a total loss. They wanted $400,000. (As I said, it was a very desirable area.) However, the few potential buyers that had come by were skeptical. Even if they bought just for the lot, they would still have the cost of scraping the existing house. Then, they'd have the problem of dealing with the lot, which because of the erosion that was taking place, might be unbuildable.

Enter Rita. She spent several days at the site checking out the building. It was still solid, though cosmetically cracked in many areas. The part that was jutting out over space sagged, but essentially was still all together. It just had no land foundation to hold it up.

Then Rita examined the land beneath where the house jutted out. The hillside, though not very steep, just kept on going down. There was no level site below from which she could build upward with a new foundation. It seemed hopeless.

On her drive home, however, she passed some construction work on a freeway overpass. She noticed that the workers were sinking pilings deep into the ground to stabilize the structure in a soft soil area and a possible solution came to her: Why not drive pilings deep into the hillside to support the property?

Rita contacted a construction firm that specialized in such work and an engineer came out to take a look. He said that the house could be supported by slamming perhaps five pilings into the mountainside. However, his firm would want $50,000 apiece for the pilings. And then there would be extensive steel work to connect them and build a base for the house. Plus, there would be the matter of supporting the house while the work was done. Again it seemed hopeless.

However, Rita persevered. She contacted a different firm and asked about driving one very long, thick piling down into the earth and then supporting the whole back end of the house on it. The engineer from this second company spent some time making calculations and said it could be done, but the total cost including the piling, the steel supports and putting the house in place would cost around $100,000. Rita had him put his bid in writing.

Next she approached the bank and offered them $100,000 cash for the property. (She planned on using another property she owned to borrow the cash.) She reasoned that the bank would not want to give a loan on the lot. They would want to sell it outright and get it out of their system. But, would they take her lowball offer?

The bank countered at $200,000 cash. That was still half of the potential value of the lot alone, if it was buildable. However, Rita would need $100,000 for the construction work, plus $200,000 to pay off the bank. She didn't have that much. So she offered the bank $100,000 cash and another $100,000 in six months. They accepted.

The rest was whirlwind work. Rita borrowed the money she needed for the construction work from relatives and friends and had the piling dug. The crew did it in three weeks, then built a steel foundation from it to solid ground and placed the house on it.

Two months later, she not only had a buildable lot, but she had a fully built house on it! All that remained was to fix the cosmetic damage and resell.

The upshot of this story is that in this very expensive neighborhood, Rita sold for $650,000 and cleared more than $300,000 on the deal, all in less than six months.

How was it possible? The answer is that she came up with a creative solution that no one else thought of. If the original owners had conceived of a single strong piling to hold up the house, they might have saved their property. If the bank executives had thought of it, they would have saved their company a lot of money, plus potentially made a profit. But only Rita thought of it, and the rewards went exclusively to her.

Brainstorming

Although Rita figured out the answer by herself, you and I won't always be so clever or fortunate. Often we will need some creative help from others. For that reason, I strongly suggest you consider brainstorming.

If you have a dream team group (as described in Chapter 5), put the problem to them. However, be careful in your presentation. If you describe the property as a hopeless situation, others are likely to think of it that way, too. On the other hand, if you present it as a challenge with great rewards possible, your associates will put their thinking caps on and go to work.

If you don't have a dream team, then ask everyone you meet and know for help. You can describe the situation without giving the property address and thus, hopefully, not risk giving the deal away to someone who has a better idea and doesn't confide in you. Particularly ask people in different aspects of construction. It's sort of like asking a doctor for an opinion. If you ask a foot doctor, she'll tell you the answer is arch supports. Ask a back doctor and it's a brace or surgery. Ask a chiropractor and it's manipulation. In the building trades, you'll get different perspectives from general contractors, engineers and specialty contractors. The thing is, one of them may just come up with a creative solution no one else considered. And you could be on your way.

Finding the creative solution is often the answer to turning a catastrophe into an opportunity. If you can do it, you too can enter the ranks of those elite entrepreneurs who make fortunes on fixers. On the next page are some guidelines to consider when you're looking for the creative solution.

Contact experts in the field who have done the work before and can assure you that your solution will fly. Then, get them to put it in writing. The last thing you want to do is buy a property based on an idea for creatively fixing it up, only to find that your hoped-for solution was actually a pipe dream.

Can You Execute?

What it all eventually comes down to is execution. You can have the best property and the perfect solution. But if you can't execute, you can't make the deal.

Executing means being able to buy (or at least tie up) the property, get the necessary work done including all of the permits, and then resell for the anticipated profit. Fall down on any of these steps and you could easily lose instead of make money.

Guidelines for Finding the Creative Solution

1. Try to work with expensive properties. As we've noted before, there's more potential profit to be made in higher-priced properties. This is particularly the case when there's one big problem to be solved.

2. When you learn that all the current thinking suggests that there's no answer, try gaining a different perspective. Brainstorm with your dream team or with anyone else who can even remotely understand the problem and pose a solution. There's simply no telling from whom you might get a workable, creative solution to your problem.

3. Make sure your solution is viable. The trouble with many creative answers is that they are untested. Yes, it may *seem* like it will work, but will it truly?

Buying the Property

In the second section of this book, we discussed various methods of buying a handyman's special that you can apply in the vast majority of cases. However, a property with a big problem can pose special difficulties that you might not run into elsewhere. For example, in our story above, Rita could not get financing of any kind on the property she wanted to buy because of its obvious problem. Even the bank that held it as an REO refused to finance it.

This can be the case with a "big-problem" property. If the house is falling down the hillside, partly burned, off its foundation because of an earthquake or a hurricane or otherwise damaged in such a way as to be uninhabitable (the key word), chances are no regular lender will give you a mortgage on it. If that's the case, you need to finance it in a different fashion.

Here are some methods of irregular financing that you may want to consider if you have a "big-problem" property:

---

*S*pecial Financing Methods for Big Problems

1. In our example, Rita financed the property on her own. She borrowed against another piece of property for the purchase money price, and then borrowed from relatives for the fix-up money. While this was hard money borrowing, it also provided her with an advantage: she didn't have to give any of the ultimate profits away in order to secure the loans. If you're faced with coming up with the money yourself, don't overlook any of the possibilities, including equity financing on another property, credit card loans and personal loans from friends and family.

2. Another alternative is a hard money loan from a private or institutional lender. These people loan strictly on the value of the property, regardless of condition. Be warned, however, that even they will falter when the lot itself is in trouble, as in our example. And be prepared to pay very high interest rates.

3. Don't forget about real estate capital venture money, available almost everywhere. What this means, however, is that you, in effect, take in a partner. Your partner puts up the money you need. In exchange,

---

you do two things. You guarantee to repay the money no matter what ultimately happens in the deal. And you agree to give your partner a percentage of the profits, if any, when the deal finishes. Sound like a rip-off? It is, but if you need the money and it's the only way you can get it . . .

Real estate venture capitalists hang around large real estate brokerage offices, title insurance offices and some small lenders. Talk to people in real estate and almost surely one or more will know of someone who will loan on any property, for a price.

4. Take in the seller as a partner. We've already discussed this in detail (see Chapter 8).

Getting the Work Done

We've already talked about doing the work yourself versus hiring it out. (If you're not sure, reread Chapter 11.) However, with a "big-problem" fixer, there's the additional difficulty of getting approval of government agencies for the work you have planned. This can be far more difficult than it may first appear to be.

Consider Rita's case. Houses in her area are generally built in two ways. Either there's a peripheral foundation and a slab, or there's a full foundation and a wood floor. Occasionally, the house is jacked up on piers or supports in a hillside situation. But, almost never are pilings used (the kind that are sunk deep into the ground).

The problem here is that while the building and safety department (which issues permits) knows about the usual kind of building, they don't know about the less-usual type. That means that they are going to be skeptical and hard to convince. They are going to want to see engineering reports.

They will want reasonable explanations about how you plan to move heavy equipment in and out. They will want to be reassured about noise. In short, in order to get the work done, you're going to have to have all your ducks in order. You're going to need to be able to answer all sorts of questions and provide massive documentation. And even then, it may take months to get approval.

Plus, there are always the neighbors to deal with. Neighbors don't like noise, dust, mess or confusion. They want to be able to quietly enjoy their property. When you do work, you are almost certainly going cross them. So, you had best be prepared for it.

How Should You Deal with Neighbors?

One entrepreneur I know who does a lot of fixers that involve heavy construction work, makes it a point to visit all the surrounding neighbors before any work at all begins. He introduces himself, explains that he's going to be fixing up the neighboring property so that it won't be an eyesore anymore. And he explains that he'll do it as quietly and with as little mess as possible. But, he tells the neighbors, if they find the noise is too loud or there's a problem, to come see him right away and he'll do his best to correct it.

My friend accomplishes two things in this way. First, he introduces himself and becomes a person and a face to the neighbors, so that when things go wrong, they're likely to say, "Oh, that's Paul's house work. He's okay. It'll be over in a few days."

Or, if they're really unhappy, they call *him* . . . instead of the city or the county or the police. That way, he has first chance at solving whatever the problem might be. It's something you may consider doing as well, even if your fixer job doesn't involve a great deal of noisemaking or fuss.

When You Don't Contact the Neighbors

There is a corollary here. I once had a friend, Joey, who bought a fixer, didn't go around to meet his neighbors and didn't bother getting a permit. Instead, he worked round-the-clock on his property. It didn't take long before angry neighbors complained to the city. The city discovered the work was taking place without permit. They immediately shut Joey down. Not only did they require he get a permit, but they seemed to evaluate his plans more strictly than for others. They also put stringent work times on him. In short, they hounded him until the work became a nightmare—a bad dream he could have avoided by taking the appropriate precautions early on.

Reselling at a Profit

Presumably by the time you get ready to resell, you've cured the problem. However, to protect yourself, you should disclose what the problem was and how you fixed it.

For example, I knew a builder whose specialty was stabilizing houses in an area of extensive mudslides. The truth is, the homes should never have been built where they were. However, they were and they kept sliding down hillsides and across washes every rainy season. He made a fortune buying them up, fixing them up and then reselling.

However, when he resold, he told every buyer that the house had slipped, that the soil was not stable and that he had attempted to stabilize the house in the soil. He provided highly technical engineering explanations that showed what he had done, which included forcing a special cement-like solution into the soil and driving steel pins deep into the earth. My friend wanted to be absolutely sure that no buyer could ever come back later on, if the house slipped again, and say he hadn't been informed of the risk.

With full disclosure, however, the danger was that potential buyers would be scared away. To get around this problem, this builder offered a limited warranty. He said that if there was any slippage within three years, he would fix it free. If slippage occurred after three years, he would pay for two-thirds of it the fourth year, one-third the fifth, and none after that. His warranty, however, was not transferable if the buyers wanted to resell.

He never seemed to have a problem reselling. Would-be buyers seemed to feel that if he was willing to warranty the house for three years, it would probably be there forever. Besides, most didn't plan to stay there forever, but instead planned to resell.

Most of his fix-ups worked fine and the houses never slipped again. But, the soil being the way it was, a few did. I don't know how those owners handled it, but I do know that they never came back complaining to the builder.

When you resell a property that has had a major problem fixed, disclose the details. If necessary, work out a warranty program.

---

*C*aution

Never try to hide a problem that you fixed or how you fixed it. Yes, chances are nothing will come of it anyway and by not mentioning it you may secure a quicker sale. But, if by some bad luck the next owners do discover the problem and the fix and, what's worse, find that the problem has returned, be prepared for a very unpleasant phone call. There's not much worse than being forced to pay for damages to a property you don't own anymore.

"Big-problem" fixers are great because they usually offer the chance at making big profits. But be careful: Identify the problem, figure a creative way to fix it and execute your plan, including a safe resale. Then you can truly enjoy your rewards.

CHAPTER 14

Getting Started

Okay, you've read this book and you know a lot about fixer-uppers. But so far your knowledge is all theoretical. Yes, you've got a lot of ideas. But what do you do first? How do get started in the field?

I can only tell you how I got started and how others I know did it. Most of us seem to have done it the same way. It was nothing difficult, complicated or secret. But, it did take some time.

For most of us, getting started happened as almost an accident. In my case, I was looking for a home/investment. I wanted to buy a house that I could move into and that I could resell in a few years for a profit. Along the way I kept running into properties that needed work. It didn't take long before I put two and two together and realized I could maximize my profits by buying a fixer.

Another person now working in the field was a mortgage broker. She had occasion to learn of properties that were being taken back by lenders. She went out of her way to look at these properties and when she found one that was particularly run down, she'd make an offer. A few of her offers got accepted.

Another individual working the field is a dentist. He made friends with some people at a title insurance company. Whenever his friends got word of a probate or trust sale, they would let him know. He would check out the property and if it seemed appropriate, make an offer.

Yet another person worked for the highway department. He subscribed to a news service (available in most communities—check with a title insurance company for its name in your area) that listed foreclosures and REOs. He checked them out.

Other people I know work closely with real estate agents. When agents learn of a potential fixer, they call up. Then it's just a matter of checking out the property and making the offer. The agents, of course, love this because they get a quick and often easy commission.

In short, there are all kinds of avenues into the handyman's special field. However, the one requirement is that you must work at it. No, you don't have to put in 40 hours a week or even 20. But, if you spend fours every weekend looking at properties, within six months you should see a great many potential fixers.

Besides, it's fun! My wife and I often make a morning or afternoon of it. We get out there and see what's available. Sellers and agents are always cordial. And there's the excitement of the hunt because there's hardly a time that goes by that we don't find at least something with potential.

In short, what you must do is get active. A fixer isn't likely to land in your lap. You have to get out there and look for it. You have to spend some time (not necessarily a lot of time) working at it.

My suggestion is that you pick a good neighborhood near where you live and "farm" it. Farming, in real estate parlance, is what agents do to get listings. They pick a neighborhood and then send out flyers, go door-to-door, make calls and do whatever else they can think of to become known to the residents. In the long run, they hope their efforts will generate many listings for them. The neighborhood becomes their listing farm.

Do the same thing with fixers. Pick a nearby geographical area (you want it nearby because once you find something, you don't want to be traveling long distances to work on it). Get to know it like the proverbial back of your hand. Get to know the streets where the older properties are, the newer tract homes with problems, the streets where water erosion or flooding sometimes takes place. Get to know those locations where fixers are likely to occur and become familiar with the typical problems they offer.

Also get to know the agents in the area. Go out with them and be sure they understand that you're ready to move if they find something suitable. You may not get a call from an agent for months, and then suddenly she is on the line with a great opportunity property.

Also get to know lenders in your area. There's no reason you can't drop in and ask to see the person who handles REOs. I do it all the time. In large institutions, I'm usually referred to a central office. In smaller ones, I sometimes end up talking to the bank president!

The bottom line, to reiterate, is to get active. Take the little time it takes and make the small effort required. Touch enough bases and you'll score!

INDEX